The
YELLOW HONEYSUCKLE
is the
SWEETEST

The
YELLOW HONEYSUCKLE
is the
SWEETEST

*Hunting, Fishing, and Journeys
with Family, Friends, and Nature*

BILL FENTRESS

FOREWORD BY WILL PRIMOS

Copyright 2021 by William C Fentress.

All rights reserved. No part of his book may be reprinted or reproduced or utilized in any form or by any electronic, mechanical, or other means, now known or hereafter invented, including photocopying and recording, or in any information storage or retrieval system without permission in writing from the author.

All inquiries should be addressed to:
William C. Fentress
PO Box 525
Bayboro, NC 28515

Ebook 979-8-9855598-0-4
Paperback 979-8-9855598-1-1
Hardcover 979-8-9855598-2-8

Manufactured in the United States of America

DEDICATION

This book is dedicated to those who helped instill and nourish in me the passion for hunting, fishing, and other outdoor sports and who set examples for the right ways to do it—Mom, Daddy, Alf, Granddaddy, Uncle Simmons, and the men and women I grew up around. It is presented in honor of the many friends with whom I have shared these experiences and who have blessed me with their presence in duck blinds, swamps, hedgerows, woods, fields, creeks, rivers, and boats. It is a thank you to my wife, Susan, who has enjoyed the outdoors with me, supported my passion, and inspired in me the decision to write, beginning 21 years ago. Finally, it is a gift to my daughter, Sarah, who with God's grace, was our greatest gift.

In memory of Richard Hudson—one of my Partners.

CONTENTS

Foreword by Will Primos	ix
Preface	xiii
There'll Be Other Times	1
As Thick as I've Seen 'Em	21
Partners	35
The River Road	60
Coming Around	75
Cabins	92
Uncle Simmons	114
Thanksgiving at Granddaddy's	143
Mack	147
The Yellow Honeysuckle is the Sweetest	170
Tying Nets	190
Taking Her Place	206
My Buddy	216
October Fields	223
Signs	230
Acknowledgments	253

FOREWORD

Bill Fentress has captured with his words what makes growing up fishing, hunting, and learning from nature, an ideal childhood. Add and surround this up-bringing and time growing up with an extended God-fearing family, and you've got the formula for building and teaching an individual who will become a strong contributor to family, conservation, society, culture, and life in general. Bill has memorialized that and more in *The Yellow Honeysuckle is the Sweetest*.

Bill's gift of putting to words the sights, sounds, and feelings he experienced living on the east coast of North Carolina, made me feel as if I was right there with him. No matter where you and I called home when we were in our formative years or where we call home now—the mountains of the West, the prairies of North and South Dakota, the Gulf, or the rolling hills and Delta of Mississippi like me—you find peace and renewed energy when you spend time in God's Great Outdoors. This is the link and thread we all share. And Bill reminds us of that with each story.

Recognizing and reflecting upon all the gifts of life's lessons he received, Bill decided to memorialize these life experiences and share them with you and me so that we may all recognize and be thankful for the blessings all around us! With each short story, you will be drawn deeper as Bill recalls and reflects on those moments that shaped his life, and his love for God, making Bill the Man he is!

You will love this book as you become a part of the anticipation of the next day's adventure, as you feel the love of family (especially a grandfather), as you think of the mementos you have placed in that hunting camp or that special place that holds the memories you cherish so much . . . the same types of memories you hope your loved ones experience, feel, understand and cherish as well. You will reacquaint yourself with those special feelings you have for a relative like Uncle Simmons; you will tear up when you remember that special bond you had with a dog like Mack who gave you the memories that took both of you to create. You will understand again the gift of sharing with your children what you loved and learned as you grew up in an extended family—realizing how important those life lessons were to your becoming the person you are today.

You will recognize the moment you realized there are those special times that, "tie you to your childhood"; you will feel the appreciation you have for those who sacrificed for you long before your time so you could have a chance in a free country, and you may even come to understand there is a lot better way to describe "getting your act together" by perhaps stating that you are "getting your mess right." Finally, you may be amazed and nod in agreement when in the most important story, Bill recognizes other gifts from God, the SIGNS!

The Yellow Honeysuckle is the Sweetest will bring back your own memories. No matter if you grew up in suburbia, the big city, or a rural place, you will leave Bill's words with an even greater appreciation for all those things you saw, heard and felt while growing up and learning to live life!

All of this to say that I strongly recommend *The Yellow Honeysuckle is the Sweetest!*

I could not put it down!!!

Enjoy,
Will Primos—Conservationist & Primos Founder

PREFACE

Thank you Will.

The Yellow Honeysuckle is the Sweetest began as a brief thought during freshman English in college. That was forty-three years ago. I got one of my few As on a caricature-writing assignment and subsequently had meaningful feedback from the professor. *One day,* I thought, *maybe when I gain more relevant experience, I can write magazine articles or perhaps* a *book.* I knew it would be about my passion for the outdoors. Hunting, fishing, just being in nature, have not simply been pastimes for me. They have been important to the very core of my existence.

Forty-three years removed from freshman English, and embracing a lifetime in the outdoors, I bring to you this compilation of stories. Most all of them involve hunting or fishing experiences. A few describe other important moments as they occurred. But they are not just recollections. I try to relay how important these events have been to me and hopefully to my family. My hope is that you will see some of you in these words. Perhaps you will remember that relative that introduced you to the outdoor sports, or maybe you will recall that extraordinary morning in the woods or marsh that filled every sense in your brain. Perhaps you will reminisce about that special bird dog. Perhaps you will find kinship in the benefits of raising your children with a certain grounding only the outdoors can provide. My hope is that my stories resound, reflect, and reverberate your own memories . . . with maybe a chuckle or a tear.

The last story was my most difficult to write and is somewhat different from the others. I struggled with it for months. I limped along, put it down, then rewrote it. Please don't jump ahead like I too would probably be tempted to do. It has its time . . . and that time is at the end. I hope it also relays to you what some of us who live into late middle-age have discovered . . . uniquely honed by our time in nature.

I have truly enjoyed all these experiences you are about to know. They are all true. They are all significant moments. The names are real . . . these are a few of the many people that I have been blessed to know over the years. If you are young, cherish your time spent hunting and fishing and enjoying nature, and create your own memories. The time spent is worth it. If you are past the halfway mark, my hope is that you find a nugget or two that will bring back that special memory tied up in the honeysuckle of your past.

There'll Be Other Times

My first real deer hunt with Granddaddy was not actually the first time I had accompanied him into the woods and marshes of Pamlico County in pursuit of the whitetail. Like all of my cousins, I'd done that several times. But during all previous hunts, I simply stood beside him and listened for the dogs, so I could describe to him their hot-trail yipping, and cold-trail bawling. Most importantly, I needed to convey the direction they were chasing the deer. He relied on me to accurately relay this information to him, so he could predict where a buck might cross a nearby logging road—giving him an opportunity to put some meat on the table.

Granddaddy had been partially deaf since he'd gotten a severe ear infection while serving in the Coast Guard in his early twenties. Each of his four children and most of his seven grandchildren served as his ears at least once. Accordingly, we'd each been baptized into the traditions of hunting deer with dogs in eastern North Carolina. It was a necessary passage for all of us; some tolerated it and some—like me—much preferred going with Granddaddy rather than staying at home and playing.

This hunt with Granddaddy was the first time I carried a gun myself while accompanying the man who had not only taught me how to shoot, but who had also instilled in me the rigid protocol of how to safely handle firearms. It was a day I'd anticipated for years. Finally, during the fall of my twelfth year, Mom felt I was ready.

When Granddaddy called that Thursday night in 1972 to invite me to go with him on Saturday, my plans quickly shifted from the usual weekend hunt for bushytails on the family farm to white, black, and tan baying hounds, clanging pickup trucks, white wooden skiffs, spongy salt marshes and the older men who hung around the fish house reposing on wooden drink crates swapping stories about politics, the war, or the weather. That was the stuff that made up a hunt in Hobucken, and a November Saturday with Granddaddy. All day Friday in school, I couldn't even begin to concentrate on history, math, or any of the other seventh grade subjects. Nor did I even notice the cute girls that sat across the classroom. I was focused intently on Saturday and how I would meticulously prepare for it Friday night which, of course, would be almost as fun as the hunt itself.

Friday night, I began the ritual by cleaning the old Winchester Model 24 double barrel shotgun that had been my father's quail gun. Only a few weekends before, Mom had retrieved it from her closet—where it was stored in its brown vinyl case—and let me shoot it for the first time. Before Mom married my stepfather, I used to gaze at its worn darkened steel barrels as it stood propped up beside her bed, knowing it could not be touched for risk of losing all BB gun privileges.

Following me in the truck as I walked down our farm road and practiced shouldering the old gun and swinging on the flushing larks, Mom encouraged me through the window. "You handle that gun naturally," she proclaimed. Mom always knew what to say to make me feel good. It was the first time the shotgun had been shot since my father's death ten years earlier. Seeing the old Winchester probably brought back some special memories for her too.

After gingerly placing the double in the gun rack, I checked my survival kit, carefully assembled after reading an article in one of my many hunting magazines. A boy never knew when he might be put into a situation like the men in *Sports Afield* and forced to start a fire with a candle, catch fish with a hand line, build a lean-to for shelter in case of a sudden snowstorm, or even use a mirror to signal a plane so he could be found. I was prepared if that ever happened to me. Using the Ouachita stone I'd ordered from the big Herter's catalog, I carefully honed my Ka-Bar hunting knife, and placed it on the desk next to the binoculars Granddaddy had given me. Two boxes of buckshot were positioned next to the knife, new split-leather laces were strung into my green knee-high rubber boots, and my red and black flannel shirt and jeans were folded over the desk chair. Finally, I retrieved the olive drab army surplus coat out of the closet and draped it over the doorknob. *Ready*. I told mom and my stepfather good night before climbing into bed with two of my favorite magazines. I read every available article on deer hunting, and even one describing how a man in the Yukon survived a grizzly attack. I'm not sure what time I finally fell asleep, but it was after much tossing and turning, and more than one look at my alarm clock.

At 7:30 a.m. the next morning, Grandaddy pulled in front of the house in his green 1970 Impala. As confirmed by the hundreds of pecan tree sap stains on the roof and trunk, he hadn't washed it since he bought it two years earlier—nor had he cleaned the interior. Mom used to kid him that if he could just find a way to keep water on the floorboards and throw in some 10-10-10, he could get a really good corn yield. Those comments were usually met with an affirmative grunt from Granddaddy.

Walking carefully to the passenger side, I made absolutely sure that my shotgun was pointed in a safe direction every single second. I was always safe, but I paid extra-special attention to it that morning. Grandaddy taught me everything about shooting safety and I never wanted to disappoint him.

"Hi Granddaddy," I said, as I opened the door and got in; I didn't want to act as excited as I felt. The hunters that raised me did not get excited. Proper etiquette was always followed at all times, even though we all knew that secretly we really did get excited.

"Hey Bud," he responded, moving his shotgun over on the bench seat, so I could put my double barrel next to it. "Toss your lunch in the backseat. We might just eat a snack at Ralph's. We'll see," he added, as I shut the door.

I was adorned in my Sears jeans, flannel shirt, army coat and green rubber boots with the Ka-Bar strapped to my belt right beside the survival kit. Granddaddy wore his familiar tattered canvas hunting pants over his black dress pants, a white dress shirt and gray sweater vest under his tan hunting coat; he also wore black dress shoes encased by his galoshes, and a faded brown duck cap. The neatly cropped snowy hair peeking out under the sides of his cap contrasted with his creviced brown skin, steel-blue eyes, and the yellow corn cob pipe in his mouth.

He never wore just plain hunting pants and coat, nor hunting boots of any kind. His attire was planned so he could quickly and efficiently shed his outer clothes, then settle right back down at his office. Many times, Grandaddy wore a tie under the outer garments.

I was itching to go, but Granddaddy was in his usual speed—which seemed practically stationary to a twelve-year-old boy. He leaned back in the bench seat and methodically cleaned out his corncob pipe with his over-filed Case pocketknife. Then, he tapped the cob part on the ashtray two or three times, dumping some of the ashes into the tray but most onto the growing pile on the floor. Next, he tipped forward and took a Dutch Masters cigar from the box on the dash, cut off a third of one, neatly stuffed it into the cob part and tamped it down with his right index finger as he held the pipe in his left hand. After he struck a kitchen match on the dash, he held it to the pipe and began puffing to get the fire going. When he got smoke, he waved the match out and tossed it in the general direction of the ashtray—and missed, adding another to the ever-growing pile on the floor. The whole car smelled of Dutch Masters and lit kitchen matches. Those wafting aromas were as familiar to me as Granddaddy himself, captured in my first memories of him hugging my sister and me as we ran to his front door.

In addition to the two-year-old pile of dirt on the floor, a smothering layer of dust covered the dash. Overlooked cigar ashes cluttered the seat, while a mess of ever-present rubber bands hung on the gearshift, placed there every day by Granddaddy as he unwrapped his business mail while sitting in his car at the post office. The car was its usual 90 degrees, so I took off my coat and laid it next to my lunch and over Granddaddy's black wool coat that always covered the .22 in the backseat.

Only seven years earlier, Grandaddy taught me all about shooting, guns, and safety with that single shot .22. Whenever Mom and I visited, I'd beg him to shoot with me. He always said yes, and with some grunting, he'd get up from his chair and slowly amble out into the backyard with me at his side carrying the rifle. Next to the woodpile, he'd fashion a target out of a torn envelope, then whittle a peg to affix the target onto a cardboard box. Granddaddy stood behind me many afternoons firmly encouraging me.

"Now Billy, line up that front post in the groove on the rear sight, and put the whole picture on the target. Squeeze the trigger. Don't yank it," he instructed, as I listened intently. It took me some time to grasp the "squeeze" part of the instructions, but when I did, I finally understood what he had been talking about and I started hitting targets much more often.

Granddaddy never paid that much attention to my accuracy, but he was always paying attention to where that muzzle was pointed, and he let me know it. "If you don't handle that gun safely, we'll put her up," he warned. I always did, except once. The only time I ever pointed any type of muzzle at Granddaddy was Christmas 1965. That year, I got toy six guns and a complete cowboy outfit with holsters, and on Christmas day when Granddaddy came down to our house to see what Santa brought, I ran to meet him at the door. "Bang, Bang, Granddaddy . . . I got you!" I proudly shouted.

He glared at me, hesitated, and then admonished, "Didn't I tell you not to point guns at anybody?" Then he walked by me without another word. Later, everything was fine, and we had a great Christmas dinner, but he had made his point.

"That gun loaded?" he asked, as he glanced down at my shotgun nestled next to his Winchester automatic.

"No sir," I quickly responded.

"That Carroll's bird gun?" Granddaddy asked.

"Yes sir," I responded. "I killed a squirrel with it the other day," veering about as far down Braggin Road as I dared.

"It'll kill a deer I reckon . . . Are you ready?" he asked.

"Yes sir," I answered. I turned and waved goodbye to Mom, who was standing on the front steps. Then we drove off toward Uncle Ralph's—two hunters, grandfather and grandson, seventy years apart in age, but equal in anticipation of the day.

Uncle Ralph owned a seafood business and store on the banks of the Inland Waterway, or "the canal" as everyone called it around home; it was the place where men gathered before and after the hunt. He had the dogs, the walk-in cooler room for the deer and, inside the store, myriad snacks for lunch. Uncle Ralph had been a hard-core hunter his entire life. Most days between November and January, you could find him listening to the hounds with his Browning rifle ready at his side. During the 1930s, he and Uncle Harmon, Granddaddy's other brother, had even guided Babe Ruth on some duck hunts. Somewhere, there was an autographed picture to prove it. Uncle Ralph wore knee-high leather-top L. L. Bean boots, tan canvas pants, a tan coat buttoned at the top and a brown canvas cap. He owned at least twenty deer dogs and as we drove up, every single one of them serenaded us with the constant boom of howls, barks, yips, and yelps.

Finally, somebody who was excited as I am! I thought.

"Where are we going?" asked Granddaddy through the car window, as Uncle Ralph battled the whipping tails, scraping paws, bellowing and general anarchy of seven or eight ready-to-hunt hounds being forced into the temporary confinement of a dog box. "Down the road to Middle Bay. The boys said they saw some fresh tracks down there early this morning. We got a couple skiffs coming up from the creek."

"We'll see you there," came Granddaddy's reply. So was the greeting between two brothers, who had enjoyed the outdoors together their whole lives, beginning in the nineteenth century. They had hunted with hounds, shot bears, sat for hours in the dove fields, watched wave after wave of canvasbacks and blackheads fly into Jones Bay, chased rabbits with beagles and waited on squirrels under water oaks. They had smoked mullets over coals and fried spot on the banks of Ditch Creek. They had worked the tongs and dredges when there was an inexhaustible supply of oysters in the Sound. Afterwards, each settled into his respective business; Uncle Ralph, a buyer of fish from local watermen; and Granddaddy, an insurance man and farmer with mules. Granddaddy and his brother had done many things, but even though both were now over seventy-five, they still had that stirring of excitement before a day's hunt and were anxious to get out there. Just like them, I was beginning to understand that pre-hunt feeling; it is one I know quite well now.

We left Uncle Ralph's, crossed the drawbridge, drove to the end of the pavement, stopped at the edge of the dirt road that led to Drum Creek and Middle Bay, and waited with the other men. None of us wanted to disturb any tracks before Uncle Ralph arrived with the dogs. The wide burlap-colored expanse of needle rush that was the meandering head of Drum Creek stretched out in front of us, and the smell of salt mud and crab pots stacked beside the road was thick. It was a cool morning. The sun was rising to the east, its brilliance reflecting off the heavy mist that was slowly relinquishing its hold on the day. The dampness and heavy air would be good for the dogs. The marsh itself was still and life in it not yet disrupted, except for a few redwings fluttering from bush to bush. Its serenity contrasted sharply with the clambering of truck doors, handshaking, hellos and the crackle of the new CBs some of the men had just bought so they could communicate while following the dogs that were chasing the deer. Granddaddy didn't care much for the radios. "You oughtta be able to tell where the deer is going yourself!" he confidently exclaimed, while emanations from his corncob pipe hovered around him like mosquitoes on Goose Creek Island in July.

"Let's go on across the head of the creek to those pines. That's where the freshest tracks were," came Uncle Ralph's advice, as he arrived to join us.

With the order given, all the trucks loaded up and we started across the marsh road toward the stand of pines near the Bay, where the deer frequently bunched up to rest on the higher ground of the pine hummocks. Once we got to the pine stand, all the trucks stopped behind Uncle Ralph. Everybody got out to look at the tracks, including Granddaddy and me. With me appropriately at his side, struggling desperately to restrain every inch of twelve-year-old boyness in my body, Granddaddy shuffled slowly up to where most of the tracks crossed the road, bent over, and peered down at them with the other men.

"Looks like a big buck. I'd say he made 'em just before daybreak," Grandaddy said, as he cupped his right hand over his right ear, fully expecting a response. And he got one.

"I reckon so, Mr. Alfred," agreed one of the men.

Just then, seven or eight hounds were cut loose from Uncle Ralph's truck and commenced to dart right, zag left, jump in front of the truck, scramble to the back of the truck and run over, through, and into each other. For about a minute, it was pure deer-dog pandemonium. Then one of them hit a track and let loose a shrill scream, signifying his primeval recognition of game scent. And they were off. Quickly, they disappeared toward the east into the pines, while some of the men scrambled into the trucks to follow. I wanted to do the same right then, but one glance at Granddaddy told me we would sit.

What on earth are we doing? Why are we not going? I wondered. It made absolutely no sense at all. But as a boy growing up in rural eastern North Carolina back then, you learned to reserve your reactions so as not to be made a fool of. I kept quiet.

"You listen now and tell me when the dogs change direction," Granddaddy instructed.

Twenty minutes later, the dogs shifted and started back west toward the head of the creek . . . and toward us. I reckoned there was a reason that old men sat while young boys fidgeted.

"Granddaddy," I said loudly. "They switched to the southwest."

"Get in, Billy. We'll catch 'em at the bridge over Drum Creek."

We arrived, as hunters in one of the boats radioed to the men already at the bridge that the deer had swum the creek and was heading our way. But by now, the road was lined with men with rifles, and we only had shotguns.

"We'll stay here in the car," Granddaddy directed, leaning back in his seat.

Good grief! How are we going to kill anything sitting here? I thought. "Okay Granddaddy," I responded.

All the men started to get active and began pointing out across the marsh, looking through their scopes and nodding to each other. All I could do was roll down the window, look out and try to catch a glimpse of something—anything. Finally, I saw him as he hightailed it to higher ground, staying low and barely detectable about 200 yards from the bridge. None of the men even got a shot.

"Where are the dogs?" Granddaddy asked.

"They're heading on up the creek, outta sight," I said, regretting that nobody even got a shot.

"You boys going over to Campbell's Creek next?" Granddaddy asked one of the men near the car, already moving on in his efficient been-there-done-this-before mind.

"I imagine so Mr. Alfred," came the reply.

Okay, let's roll right now! I wished to myself.

But once again, Granddaddy was on Granddaddy time. Like a sloth basking in a time warp, he methodically cleaned his pipe, ground down a piece of cigar in it, lit it with a kitchen match and cut his eye over at me as he drew smoke. I swear it seemed like thirty minutes. "Let's go on up to Campbell's Creek Billy."

"Yes sir," I agreed.

As we crossed the Inland Waterway drawbridge leaving Goose Creek Island, there was a couple of large yachts to the north motoring toward us—snowbirds, no doubt. *Nice boats, but I'd rather have a new bolt-action .22 rifle with a Weaver scope,* I thought. Granddaddy, an oysterman at heart despite his years shrouded in insurance renewals, did not even look at them as he turned right onto Campbell's Creek Road and headed north. We drove close to three miles and turned left onto a logging road that had been cut into Gum Swamp only four years earlier. That road was a big deal back then. It was three miles long and had been built by a timber company to extricate large cypress and junipers. When I was seven, Uncle Ralph had ridden a bunch of us kids around it on a Friday afternoon, while we sat in the back of his pickup. Of course, this was after he told us about the lost hunter who'd wandered into the swamp back in the '30s or '40s, or maybe it was the '50s. I couldn't remember, but I knew that poor guy never made it out. And during that truck ride, I'd inspected each stump, bush and tree only daring to imagine him staggering from behind them at any moment. That was true wilderness to me. *And now we were going to hunt it!*

The dog truck arrived, turned up the logging road, drove out of sight and returned in a half hour. "They hit a track up there, Mr. Alfred, and started off this way!" one of the boys yelled out of the dog truck as it sped by, heading toward a spot by the road about 300 yards from where we stood.

"Billy, you get out and stand right there . . . and keep your eyes open. Let me know when you hear the dogs; wave and point to where you hear 'em. Be ready now. If he comes, he'll come fast," Granddaddy instructed.

I promptly exited the Impala and took my assigned position. Granddaddy turned in his seat, paused and looked up at me through the window. In that instant, I could see the excitement of the hunt that he still carried with him, even after his 82 Novembers.

There I was, the product of his training, dressed in full regalia with my dad's shotgun broken down at the middle, waiting for final instructions from the man who taught it all to me in the first place.

"Load your gun and be safe," he said.

"Okay Granddaddy," I replied.

He drove off, leaving me there by myself. Truth is, Granddaddy had always shown that confidence in me, like when he let me shoot the .22 alone in his yard at nine years old and climb up high in the barn loft to throw down hay to the mules with a pitchfork. He knew I was careful, mature, and trustworthy. Boys weren't meant to be coddled anyway. You either did it right or you didn't. I slid two Remington buckshot shells into the old Winchester, the familiar metallic and plastic thump echoing from the full and modified barrels. I was ready, sturdy, and staunch. "If he comes here, I'll get him . . . just like I shot that first squirrel a month ago," I told myself.

It had become one of those bright November mornings with the clear cobalt-blue sky and sharp air staking their ground against the last salvos of a bygone summer. The low pocosin woods was interspersed with large pines, red maples and sweetgums, and the straw-laden forest floor was interrupted here and there with patches of reeds. Yellow gumtree leaves and scarlet maple leaves littered the water in the canal beside the road, breaking the reflection of the overhanging pines with a menagerie of color. The smells of fall were everywhere; the earthiness of dying leaves, sweet woodiness of fresh fallen pine straw, and the faint scent of gun oil from the old double resting on my shoulder. Just down the road, Granddaddy stooped by the Impala, shotgun cradled in his arms, eyes darting back and forth scanning for any movement in the woods. He was checking back with me every other head turn.

Then I heard them—the dogs were coming, fast and hard! I jerked my head toward Granddaddy and waited until he looked my way. As soon as he did, I waved at him and hurriedly pointed to the west toward the dogs.

He waved back and gestured toward the woods, telling me in his way to keep my eyes there. The baying dogs were bearing down now, and their frantic yelping and deep moaning echoed off every gum and pine in front of me.

With each hysterical howl emanating from their bowels, my own chest heaved with excitement. My death grip on the shotgun tightened, while I searched desperately to spot any flash of brown or white amongst the trees. The dogs were getting really close now. I glanced at Granddaddy, subconsciously seeking more direction. But he had his eyes riveted on the woods, so I turned back quickly and did the same. It seemed like the dogs were going to literally jump into my lap. *That buck has to be within twenty yards!* I hurriedly checked left, right . . . up and down the road. Again, I checked the woods. And then I saw them; all seven dogs, but no deer. *Where's the buck?* I frantically examined every bush and every tree, and hastily scanned up and down the road to see if he had crossed. *No deer.* The hounds banked hard to my left, bounding over each other toward Granddaddy, mouths gasping for air between each bellow. I waved at Granddaddy, but his eyes were riveted to the woods.

As quickly as they had appeared, the pack was gone—bounding away from me and Granddaddy.

After he knew they'd passed, Grandaddy looked my way as I reluctantly began to walk toward him. "Did you ever see that deer?" he asked me, as I approached.

"No sir," I replied.

"Well, neither did I. Damn thing just vanished, I reckon."

We looked down the road at the other hunters. None raised his gun. The last of the dogs turned away and headed back west into Gum Swamp, their baying gradually becoming fainter and fainter.

"Do you hear 'em anymore?" came the predictable question from Granddaddy.

"No sir," I responded, still looking into the woods and up and down Campbell's Creek Road, the last breaths of hope escaping to the morning.

Granddaddy walked slowly to the Impala, unloaded his gun, and rested it against the front seat. "Let's go to Ralph's and get something to eat. Maybe we'll get 'em next time," he suggested.

When we arrived at Uncle Ralph's, there was a boisterous group gathered around the cooler room. "You boys have any luck?" Granddaddy asked.

"Yes sir, Mr. Alfred. We shot a small buck up at the head of Drum Creek . . . same one that crossed up there in the marsh. The dogs ran him out on Lowland Road and we got him there."

"Well, I guess we shudda gone there," Granddaddy said, turning to look at me. "We'll get one next time, Billy."

"That's okay Granddaddy," I said, opening the cooler room door to examine the deer on the floor. I had done it many times as a younger boy. Usually, I was excited and curious when I gazed at the deer in that frozen room, not knowing or caring who actually did the shooting. But this time, I was disappointed. I stared at the deer for a while before shutting the door and going inside the store to get a snack. It was the same cooler room, same group of men, same dogs, same drink crates, same stove, and we sat there and ate the same potted meat and Vienna sausages. But I was a different boy. I was different from that day forward.

After eating, Granddaddy had to get home early so he dropped me off at my house. Mom came out to meet us. "Did you have any luck?" she asked, eagerly anticipating the results as only a mother raised in a hunting family could.

"No, the dogs came close, but we didn't see him," I replied, collecting my gear.

"Don't know why we didn't see that deer, but there'll be other times," Granddaddy reassured Mom and me.

"Thanks Granddaddy, I enjoyed it," I said, as he pulled away in the Impala.

There were no other times with Granddaddy. He lost his sight in the spring of 1973 and could not hunt anymore. Mom and Uncle Alfred helped him daily in his insurance business and we always visited him on Sunday so I could feed his mules; his farm hand did not work on Sundays.

When I turned sixteen and could drive, I visited Granddaddy

myself every Sunday and sat with him an hour or more before tending to the mules. Sooner or later, we always got around to talking about hunting and I would constantly nudge him to tell his stories—like the time he and Uncle Ralph went into a dove field with twenty-five shells a piece and bet each other who would come out with more birds. For more than fifty years, Granddaddy always claimed he killed one squirrel on the way in and finished the day with that squirrel and nineteen doves.

"Uncle Ralph," he claimed, "had three doves."

Whenever I confronted Uncle Ralph about that, he would always say, "It was the other way around."

One particular Sunday when I visited Granddaddy, Uncle Ralph was there too. That was my chance to get to the bottom of the story, so I asked them about that dove hunt, the infamous bet and who was actually telling the truth. They both stalled, grinned at each other and crossed and re-crossed their legs. Granddaddy leaned over in his chair and tapped his pipe on the spittoon, while Uncle Ralph adjusted his coat and rubbed his chair arm. They both laughed, but neither would say anything. I let it drop.

There was also the time that the two brothers killed three bears, while taking a mule cart up to a field at the head of Jones Bay. One bear had come out of the woods, and they had shot him. Then two others came out and they shot them, too. They had to make two trips with the cart to get them all back home—a welcome addition to their dinner table.

Then there was a story about the moose deer. Mom was just a little girl at the time and accompanying Granddaddy when he shot a big buck on Campbell's Creek road. Back then, it was one the biggest ever shot around that area; everybody agreed it was "as big as a moose."

I knew all the old stories and relished every minute I spent with Granddaddy as he told them to me. And I knew by the twinkle in his blue eyes that he enjoyed it, too. He wasn't able to physically be there in the woods and marshes anymore, or hunt with me—other than that one time—but he could relay the excitement of all his memories and love of the outdoor sports to me. And that he did.

Forty-eight years have passed since I deer hunted that first time with Granddaddy. Since then, I have enjoyed hundreds of days in the woods and fields of eastern North Carolina, scanning white oak canopies for squirrels, crouching in ditches with doves coming in to feed, flushing quail over locked-up setters and pointers, listening for swooshing wings in the early morning marshes and sitting in stands searching each materializing shadow for my own moose deer. I only spent that one day on a real hunt with the man who taught me how to shoot and handle a gun. But today, every time I pick up a firearm, I think back to when I was a boy—and I can still hear his deep voice over my right shoulder, giving me his unwavering and stern instructions to line up the sight on that paper target with the whittled peg in the bull's-eye. "Keep that muzzle pointed in a safe direction," he always said.

I often think about how he helped instill in me a love of nature with his stories, while nurturing my self-confidence by allowing me to shoot the .22 by myself. As a parent, I now know how difficult it is to give your child that type of freedom so they can grow.

Every time I see a deer, I think of Granddaddy's love of hunting, the outdoors, and eastern North Carolina. And each time I hunt, I am thankful that I had him to pass that on to me. That first hunt in 1972 was my last with Granddaddy, but he's still with me every time I'm fortunate enough to be in the autumn woods.

As Thick as I've Seen 'Em

If you were a boy growing up in rural eastern North Carolina in the 1960s and 1970s, you probably had a chance to go dove hunting on opening day, usually the Saturday before Labor Day in early September. Typically, the temperature was 90-plus degrees with the smell of summer weeds and the husky scent of fresh-picked brown-dry corn in the air. Where I grew up, it also frequently included unrelenting molestation by hungry mosquitoes and the acrid smell of OFF! repellent. Some of the monstrous mosquitoes were big enough to be misidentified as swallows when you caught them out of the corner of your eye. Of course, we younger boys could likewise mistake the swallows for doves until they got really close.

Everybody went dove hunting: farmers, non-farmers, boys, girls, people who hunted a lot and some pilgrims who only hunted once a year. We called those folks out-of-towners. Always present and not attuned to the ways of us locals, these dit-dotters descended upon us in droves; however, very few of these invaders could be found after opening day. They'd bought their license, popped 100 shells at 60-yard birds, yahooed at each other and went home, returning to their football games for another year. You wouldn't see them in the field until next Labor Day weekend, and you certainly wouldn't see them hunting doves in the winter.

But that was not the case with the men I grew up hunting around. Most of them didn't even go dove hunting in September. Instead, they waited until the weather turned in November or December. By then, the phones of these normally conversation-efficient men began to ring. Plans were made and the fields were evaluated. They embraced the cold weather and they loved to hunt doves in the winter. And so did I. Oh yeah, I've had many enjoyable opening-day dove hunts in September, usually combined with pig pickings, potato salad, iced tea and family get-togethers. But the dove hunt I still remember the most happened in January of my fifteenth year.

That Saturday in 1975 started with a low of 25 degrees, following a cold front that had blown through the preceding Friday morning. In the frigid predawn darkness, I walked down to the river woods in hopes of spotting squirrels, but none of them wanted to brave the last remaining winds of the front. During the empty-handed walk back home, I was already wondering if we would hunt doves that afternoon. Sure enough, the phone began to ring around ten o'clock.

"Hello . . . Yeah . . . They found some birds up at Neals Creek Road? A big bunch? We got enough to shoot 'em? Okay, we'll meet you there at 11:30." My stepfather, Alf, hung up and walked into the den. "You want to go dove hunting this afternoon?" he asked me, knowing full well that I did. "Some of the boys running deer said they saw quite a few up Neals Creek Road this morning," Alf relayed with an unusual anticipation in his voice.

"What time are we leaving?" I asked.

"Let's leave about 11:15," he replied. We always got there well before the other hunters and Alf was joked unmercifully about it by the whole gang. "What in the world? You been here all night? Did Lois run ya off early?" or "He just wants to get the best spot in the field!" Sometimes, it was, "He wants to get there early so he can start eating candy!" These were just some of the typical jabs he endured once the whole group arrived and started their routine.

I went to my room and started laying out my clothes for the hunt: old Levi's, flannel shirt, brown canvas hunting coat, and the green hat with rabbit fur ear flaps. I retrieved the double-barrel from the rack on the wall, broke it open to make sure it wasn't loaded, and placed it on my desk. I loaded four boxes of Shur-Shot shells from Grandmamma's old trunk at the end of the bed into the converted plastic tackle box that was now my shell carrier. I pulled on my Red Ball boots with my jeans carefully tucked inside, as there would probably be some water in those ditches. Finally, I grabbed an extra sweatshirt from my dresser, just in case it got colder late in the afternoon.

Outside my room, I heard the door to the attic open. That familiar squeak and jiggle meant that Alf was retrieving his gear: the Browning Auto-5 without a vent rib, hip-boots and shells. "You ready?" he asked, standing in the doorway.

"Yeah, I'm coming," I replied. Grabbing all my stuff and following Alf, I headed outside to our Chevy pickup. At fourteen with your shotgun in hand, gear slung over your shoulder, and thoughts of wild game in your head, it's an exciting walk; it's also one of those subtle nuances of the hunting tradition that we all remember. I still get a tingle today when I pack all my adult accumulations into the truck for a hunt; that familiar rekindled rise in emotion that we pray still comes is a connection to the memories of our younger years, and a harbinger of what we hope will be new experiences equal to the bars set long ago.

Once we got to Bayboro, we turned up Neals Creek Road and drove all the way to the end where the gravel path led to wide open farmland. Alf pulled around to the edge of the woods on our left, stopped the truck and we both got out to scout the field on the right where we would hunt that day. I always thought that scouting may have been the reason Alf always wanted to get there early, but he never mentioned it to me. I suppose figuring out why grown men do the things they do is part of a boy's job.

The late morning sun glistened off the brown bean stubble, as the remaining remnants of frigid cold surrendered to the daily cycle. The morning wind had completely subsided and the clear blue sky reclaimed its rightful domain over the storms of the previous day. Leaning back against the Chevy, I took a deep breath and sucked it all in. It was 45 degrees and as a young man, you really feel alive on a clear cold day like that. My rigid but faded Levi's and the thick, soft flannel shirt felt clean and fresh, and my boots warmed my double-socked feet. I was excited and itching to get out there in the field. But as with all my hunting days, there was a prescribed enjoyment taken in the time spent basking in the pre-hunt routines, while also anticipating the possible experiences of the next few hours.

The usual fellows started arriving truckload by carload. Pickup trucks, Ford's, Chevys, four-wheel-drives, two-wheel drives and a few cars all announced the gang's arrival with their diesel rumblings, tailgate bangings, door slammings and the wholesome smell of steaming mud on hot mufflers. Dressed in camouflage, brown Duxback hunting coats, wool sweaters, sweatshirts, overalls, flannel shirts and even white shirts with hunting coats pulled over them, all the usual men began getting out and congregating near our truck. It was a collage of hunting paraphernalia not exactly out of today's Cabela's catalog, but it was what we wore back then. Soon, the typical haranguing began.

"I know Alf was here first. I can see the candy wrappers!" came the first salvo.

"Billy did you get any candy at all?" they asked me, acting concerned that my chocolate intake could have been affected.

"I tell you one thing, I don't believe the candy would go to waste around any of this crowd," came the predictable quick response from my stepfather.

"Did you put your flag out there at your spot Alf?" came the next shot.

"Yes, sir, I did, and don't you get near it . . . if you do, I won't give you any of Lois's fudge," came his response.

All the men chuckled. I smiled, and awkwardly shifted my apprentice eyes to the ground.

"Anybody bring Bill's bicycle?" came another retort from Alf.

Mr. Bill, one of the regulars, had a habit of walking the field all day long instead of staying put in a ditch like everyone else. One day, the men brought him an old junk bike complete with a red bow that Mom had tied.

"Use this here try-sickle, Bill. Maybe you can get around better. At least we'll be able to hear ya com'n," was the recited barb at Bicycle Presentation Day. That really got some laughs and still does today when those of us who are left talk about old times.

The fellows were just getting warmed up when Mr. Jerry broke in, "Look over there . . . good gracious!"

I looked toward the field and thirty doves dipped low over the bean cuts about ten feet above the ground—loafing, as the old men called it. Casting aside any discussions of bikes and candy, all heads turned toward the field. "They might fly early today being as cold as it is," came one prediction from somewhere in the crowd.

"Yessir," came a reply, just as another flight swept even lower across the field.

"I don't believe them birds've been shot at all," one of the older men observed, still standing with his foot on his truck bumper.

"We're going on and get in the field," one of the hunters declared, gathering up his gear and sons.

"So are we," came another response to the sight of still more birds piling into the field.

With that, the gradual and correctly unhurried but steady pace of men marching into a winter dove field began. *Let's get out there quick!* I thought.

As usual, Alf and I brought up the rear. He taught me that you just don't run out there like you don't have any sense. He never used the word *decorum*, but he knew what it meant, and he set by example its observance in any field with other dove hunters.

We would walk gentlemanly slow to our chosen spots. "I'm going to get right over there in that ditch, Billy," he said. "Why don't you go down there further another hundred and fifty yards and get in this same ditch. Nobody will be outside of us toward those woods. Keep your eyes open."

I grabbed my shell box, jacket and shotgun and started walking with Alf down the ditch bank. To our right, fifteen or so hunters marched into the field, carefully stopping at self-assigned stations and standing until everyone got situated. Proper dove hunters took care to remain clearly visible, while everybody was still picking their places; that way, everybody knew the locations of everybody else and could adjust accordingly. The whole scene was an unplanned but, nonetheless, carefully orchestrated series of movements, the result being an eastern North

Carolina dove shoot ready to happen. Each hunter was spaced at least a hundred yards apart, both up and down the ditches and between cuts. No hunter was directly opposite another. That way, you had ample shooting room but the whole field was covered by somebody within a manageable shooting range of the birds.

When everybody was sure they had their positions, we all started getting ready by easing down into our chosen ditches, breaking brush to clear our shooting areas, getting shells ready, and handling any other necessary preparations so that if the birds flew quick, we'd be ready to shoot. My ditch bank was overgrown with high switch grass and reeds, so I took ample time to clear my immediate area, tossing the debris in the bottom of the ditch to prevent me from miring down in the thick peaty mud. Finally, I loaded the old Winchester with two 8s and clicked her shut. It didn't take long.

The sun was high, the sky still unblemished, and the temperature was now just below fifty degrees—perfect dove weather. In the woods to my left, three hundred yards away, a pileated woodpecker pounded out his unmistakable rhythm on a half-rotten tree. A yellow hammer was squawking somewhere to the woodpecker's right, obviously bothered by that hammering racket and its effect on an otherwise quiet afternoon. In front of Alf and me were three cuts of harvested beans and no hunters. Behind us continued another six or seven cuts of picked beans and all the rest of the men. If the birds continued to fly as they had so far, Alf and I would have first pickins—as the old folks said. I noticed one lone dove fly across the field. *Too high.* Not surprisingly, no shots rang out. This was not a Labor Day crowd. This old-school bunch knew when to shoot and when to sit still. Looking toward the woods, I saw a big flock of twenty birds leave the trees heading directly for Alf and me. They were low, just ten feet off the ground and barely flapping their wings. I hunkered down in the ditch like I'd been taught, still looking at them with my head just above the bank. The birds in the flock shifted back and forth in their respective positions, dropping here, fluttering there, slowly dipping and raising their pointy wings, propelling themselves with grace and with little visible effort—getting closer. If you're a dove hunter, you understand how fast they can fly and how sometimes they seem to dipsy doodle when they hear you click the safety. I'm not joking. If you've hunted doves, especially winter birds that have been shot, you know what I mean. But these birds were different. They were gliding leisurely into our field. They crossed the hundred-yard mark, and I knew then I would at least get a shot at them.

Maybe today I can kill more than my usual two or three? I wondered. Waiting until I could see their eyes and hear their wings make that high-pitched whirr as they fluttered just in front of me, I rose up quickly. They didn't even change their path. Picking out the lead bird, I dropped him cold then smoothly pulled around on the second. I clearly missed him, as most of the flock flew right by my head only five feet away. As the rush of air pushed by their wings swept around me, it felt like I was within the flock myself. I'd never been that close to darting birds. Instinctively, I ducked to ensure one didn't take my hat off. The birds spread out behind me into a barrage of shotgun fire, and I saw four more fall out to the other hunters. I was thrilled to have my own bird down and the chance that this close-up shooting would continue the rest of the day was already sneaking into my mind

Still bowing my chest over my first dove, I leaned over to pick him up without even getting out of the ditch. Raised in dove fields, you're taught to keep your head on a swivel at all times, and your eyes always searching for that next bird. Just then, I looked up and spotted another flock of thirty coming straight at me again. Still, another was heading straight for Alf! I glimpsed him knock out two just before I swung on the lead bird in the group in front of me. Two birds fell out dead just outside the ditch again. *Two with one shot!* I was so fired-up, I didn't even think of pulling the second trigger on the old double. I had shot three times and had three birds. *Good night! The birds are flying thick!* I thought, imitating the older hunters in my mind.

The flocks were packed tight and there wasn't an ounce of skittishness amongst any of them. They wanted to get in that field bad and fifteen or more hunters weren't going to stop them. I reloaded just as another thirty-bird flock came out of the woods. Again, I hunkered low. But they flew straight at Alf, and he peeled out two more. Even before his second bird hit the ground, another flock dipped across the next hedgerow directly in front of me and bounded straight at me. I whiffed on those—that old nemesis of boy-excitement rearing its ugly head. *Stupid,* I thought.

• • •

The rest of the day was a steady repetition of this same scenario. Flock after flock poured relentlessly into that bean field, fiercely determined to feed without any concern for the hunters that waited. It would not have made any difference; these birds were coming to that field and coming in hard. I was shooting well for me, and my bag was growing. Still, I didn't dare let that thought enter my mind, knowing all wheels could fall off at any time.

Some of the men quickly got their limit and some evidently never got a limit, although I suspected they could have had more than twelve birds. After an hour, Alf and most of the men started walking to the trucks. It took me a while to get my twelve birds—two hours. Obviously, I had a cold spell because the doves never did stop coming. My last bird was the hardest shot of the day, a left to right screamer at thirty-five yards. Normally, I wouldn't have even taken that shot back then in my teen years. But that day I had the feeling. I put the bead on the lone dove, swung through him, obtained what I judged in my limited hunting years as the correct lead, kept swinging and pulled the first trigger on Dad's bird gun. The dove folded and fell dead fifty yards out in the cut.

Okay Billy, act like you've been there. Be a man and not a boy. That was a great shot, but don't be an idiot and awkward here, I lectured myself. I climbed out of the ditch, brushed off my jeans and began the slow triumphant walk. Kneeling down to pick up that last bird of the day, I took a moment to admire its mauve-colored feathers, the purple nuances of the tuft just in front of its wings, its fluffy pink undersides, and the bluish eyes. The iridescence of its ear feathers shimmered in the angling afternoon sun. The dove was soft and delicate, and it was difficult to imagine how such a fragile animal could fly like it did that day: headlong into repeated gunfire and straight into the memories of an almost fifteen-year-old boy.

Standing, I glanced out of the corner of my eye at the other hunters, knowing they saw me pick up my last bird, and knowing they witnessed the shot that I'd just made. It was a proud feeling, knowing grown men were watching—but it had to be handled correctly. I walked back to the ditch, picked up my spent shells, unloaded my gun and stooped down to count the birds. Although everyone could still see me, it still fit within proper decorum. I slowly counted out my twelve, stuffed them in my coat, then stood up and soaked in the moment. I then watched the remaining hunters still in the field, ducking as still more flocks flew over my spot straight into the waiting barrage. It was quite a sight.

Picking my way through the apparently unimpressed group of men swapping stories at the truck, I first loaded the old double into the cab, then lowered the tailgate and slowly began to pluck the doves out of my coat. I was anxiously waiting for somebody to acknowledge what I'd just done. One at a time, the birds were methodically placed on the truck bed: *1, 2, 3, 4, 5, 6, 7, 8.*

Finally, "How many you got there, Billy?" Mr. Jerry ventured with a wink to Alf.

"I got twelve," I said, trying desperately not to crack a smile.

"Good gracious!" came the reply. "They must've been thicker than I thought!" A bunch of winks and grins and chuckles ricocheted over the group. At that age, most boys would want something at least akin to praise for a job well done. But that kind of kidding meant I was now part of them, and I wouldn't have traded the moment for a new Browning.

"Didn't I see you get two with one shot?" came another question.

I knew it was meant as a compliment, but at the same time I suspected that the safeties had just been taken off a steel conibear.

"Yes, sir," I said.

"Of course, one of them I believe you just plain beat down with that old double barrel, they were so close to you," came the return volley.

As I stood there, fully expecting it, I took it on the chin and couldn't help but grin. There I was, getting ribbed by all of them—the men with whom I'd grown up hunting in these fields. Another one had been hooked, reeled in and added to the catch of lifelong hunters—and they knew it. They all laughed, turned and started putting up their gear.

I put my coat in the truck, hit the mud off my boots and leaned against the door. We all stood there for fifteen or more minutes petting dogs, drinking Cokes, counting birds, and watching wave after wave continue to invade the field. I heard some of the older men say it was the most doves they'd ever seen. Everyone agreed with nods, chin rubs and head scratching. I knew it was the most I'd ever seen but I was only fourteen. Still, I knew I had witnessed something remarkable, and the men were giving that thought its vindication. The thick-feathered birds had probably arrived hungry on the cold front that had blown in the day before. It would be another cold night and the doves needed to feed—and now it was time to let 'em do it.

That night, after cleaning Dad's shotgun and hanging it in the rack in my room, I read several stories about dove hunting in the magazines I'd accumulated. My very first limit was in the bag—no matter that it took four boxes; that was a minor detail. I was a dove hunter now, not just a two-bird wannabe. And my place had changed amongst the men.

Partners

Next to spouses and careers, hunting partners can be some of the most important choices we make in life. As a matter of fact, I would venture to say that many of us have spent more time ensuring our outdoor partners are of the right make up, demeanor, and character than we have spent assessing our ability to fulfill the obligations of being a good wife or husband or calculating our compatibility with a particular job description. Just ask a hunter how much he or she spends each year on flowers or gifts for their significant other or career-improving books compared to Cabela's, and you may get some real insight as to how he or she really evaluates priorities. I will leave it right there because my wife reads most of my work, and my hope is that some other spouses are reading this story. I certainly do not want any unnecessary contentious conversation started because of my pontifications. Let's just say that we all agree our spouses are important and so are our hunting partners.

I have been blessed with many partners during my sixty years, some planned and some entirely unexpected. They have been lifelong friends with whom I've hunted since childhood, and acquaintances with whom I've only shared a very few hunts but who left a mark. They have told outrageous tales, jabbed back when I threw out a little barb, cooked for me, and ate what I cooked. There is something special about hunting, that sears in place our memories with others. Maybe it's the vivid nature where our grand experiences take place or the team efforts we go through to make it all happen? Maybe it's the getting up early, the black coffee, the smell of eggs and bacon in a cabin, the swoosh of ducks over decoys or the violent uprising of a big covey followed by the delirium of released bird dogs? Maybe it's the sunrises, the sunsets, the gobbles at dawn, the split oak fires or the oysters? Maybe it's the bonds we have over lifetimes? I'm not really sure. But I do know we're blessed when these partners come into our lives.

Like many boys, my first hunting partner was a dog, Pepper. I wish I could say Pepper was the granddaughter of King Rothschild's Sire of Pepper Creek, but I cannot. Pepper was a fittingly, albeit not uniquely, named black and white pointer-mix stray who took up at Miss Jo's house in Bayboro. Somehow, through either constant brow beating with her pathetic brown eyes or via her constant hanging around the back door looking for food, Pepper convinced Miss Jo to call *me*—not my mother, her friend—but *me*.

"Billy," she commanded, "I have a beautiful dog you would just love!"

Of course, I immediately got off the phone and begged Mom to take me to Bayboro. "Miss Jo's got a dog she says I need!" I always thought Miss Jo should have led many of the sales classes I attended in my banking career. Let me tell you, she talked directly to the buyer, and went right around the secretary. I'm not sure how long it took for Mom to talk to her again, but we came home with Pepper in the Chevy wagon and me with a smile as broad as the cuff on my dungarees. Pepper was one of the smartest dogs I ever owned. She followed me everywhere—from our store to Grandmamma's house to the woods behind our house to the tractor shelter woods across the road, down Swan Point Road, and of course behind our neighbor's house. Pepper was smart enough to look both ways before she crossed the road. Don't smirk; I saw her do it a hundred times. She also knew how to be quiet as I planned a sneak-up strategy on the local robins and wrens. But her mind absolutely took the day off when it came to our neighbor's chickens.

Similar to a lot of folks when I was a boy, our neighbor had free ranging chickens, except back then we didn't call them that. We just said he didn't have a pen; most people didn't. The upside there was that the feathered little bundles got a lot of nutrients. The downside was that the chickens did not have a safe place to congregate—or in Pepper's view, an escape. Needless to say, one of those Rhode Island Reds failed to make it to the North Carolina cover bushes one day and Pepper came out with a prideful mouthful. Amid a menagerie of flying feathers, cackling, and wild animalistic pursuit that would have made any cheetah's spots turn to stripes with envy, I looked on in horror, as our neighbor bolted out of the house and predictably and understandingly started hollering. He was upset and so was I, except I was more upset because one of the premier cedar waxwing and robin-shooting bushes east of the Mississippi was about to go the same route as Pepper's chicken.

I told him I was sorry, corralled Pepper and slunk off back to our country store, hoping my hunting privileges had not been affected. I wasn't in the store five minutes when Mom got the call. She looked at me, as she relayed our neighbor's comments. Always the gentlemen to me and Mom, he simply asked that Pepper not be allowed back in his yard. "It's fine for Billy to keep hunting birds."

Mom and I knew a deal when we saw it. I promised Mom that Pepper would not set foot in that specific yard ever again. From then on, she stopped at Grandmamma's yard and waited for me to return, cedar waxwings, robins or sparrows in hand. Then, we'd proceed on to the next hunting location.

I've enjoyed the companionship of several bird dogs and a few Labs, but none were as staunch as Pepper when she sat waiting at the edge of Grandmamma's yard, the temptations of scurrying ground-dwelling delicacies just yards away. More than once, my salivating Lab Luke pounced from my side into a mess of mallards swimming just inches away as the first of the morning's incoming flocks circled overhead. Likewise, my setter Mack jumped point every once in a while, flushing coveys fifty yards ahead. But Pepper never broke. I suppose I should have trained all my dogs on our neighbor's chickens.

Pepper finally passed away from heartworms when I was ten, but for two years—a lifetime for a young boy—we were inseparable. Mornings under the cedar waxwing bushes were never the same after she left.

Sitting on the counter in our renovated old store, there is a picture of Pepper and me with both of us sitting in a double rocker. I'm dejected and sulking because Mom told me "No" to some forgotten request, and I am mistakenly thinking that my feigned consternation might help me get my way. Just like me, Pepper is pouting too. For some reason only known to mothers, Mom was laughing at the time she took that picture, which made me even more ill. I kicked my leg out stiff and stomped the floor to show my nine-year-old exasperation—and Pepper looked over, agreeing with me in her boy's-best-friend way. To this day, it is my favorite picture of myself. Thank God for first dogs, and intuitive mothers.

As I matured into a young man in my twenties, one of my best friends, Marvin, and I began to quail hunt together. I had my own dogs by then and we both still had a burning desire to get out and chase Mr. Bob like we'd done in our formative years with our father and stepfather.

Marvin and I had known each other since kindergarten, so our history—which included grade school, high school and playing tackle and guard side-by-side for three years—gave us a treasure of rich histories to throw at each other across a hedgerow as Mack and Missy sniffed out all the nooks and crannies. Invariably, during our hunts, I reminded Marvin to check his boots to ensure they were tied when we plodded through briars.

"Let me know if you need help!" I prodded. I was never sure he'd ever learned to tie his shoes because the one day we were taught to tie shoes in kindergarten, his mother—ever aware of distinguished dress—had sent him out of the house in polished loafers. I can still see Marvin, sitting there trying to learn to tie shoes on the Mother Goose shoe, or was it the Old Woman Who Lived in the Shoe's shoe? Well, whoever lived in the shoe—it was her shoe that he tried to tie—I think I probably told him right there at five years old, "Don't worry, I'll never bring it up again."

Of course, for every allusion to his shoe tying he would offer his own retort. "Well," he replied, "you look out for ants over there 'cause I can't stand the sight of you doing another jig in your skivvies!" This attempt at jocular retort referred to my crossing a ditch one day when we were quail hunting. Crawling out the other side, I inadvertently put my knee right smack dab in a pile of fire ants. If you've ever done that, you understand they start letting you know immediately that you've messed up.

I put the Browning Auto 5 down, dropped my pants to the ground and started slapping here and dancing there. With Wrangler hunting pants at my knees and boxers flapping in the wind, I was doing my absolute best Jed Clampett clod-hopping, boot-scooting, impression right there in the middle of the dirt road. I would have laughed myself if the little red bastards hadn't been eating my tail off. Amongst Marvin's roaring, I think I even detected a grin on Mack's rust and white muzzle, as he checked back to see what all the commotion was about. He probably thought, *Dang, I'll never get anything with this crowd! Maybe I can get on at a south Georgia plantation somewhere?* The guffawing could have been heard all the way to Raleigh. I just don't understand why a man, or dog for that matter, would relish so in my unenviable position—getting stung all over my most sensitive areas and having to undress in the middle of a dirt road far off the beaten path. Lot of nerve right there. But Marvin had that nerviness. He even reneged on a bet one time. Just because I made the unsurpassed mistake of asking him to return to the truck from a full twenty yards away to lock his door after we had already started after the dogs, he kept bugging me to bring my "dust laden" checkbook into the twentieth century and spend some money on some power door locks. His whining was so feverish, you would have thought I had busted a covey or not supplied any of the dogs or any of the places to hunt.

Knowing I was about to buy a new truck in '96, I offered a deal to him "If I buy a truck with power door locks, will you please contribute and buy a duck boat?"

"Certainly!" he responded. "No problem!"

Well, that was the first duck boat I ever saw fit onto a woman's ring finger. "Sorry bud," he said, "but that ring finger took precedent over a duck boat."

Ain't that something? A friend of thirty years doing a bud that way? In my single days, I didn't understand that at all. I thought he was getting as flighty as some of the girls who didn't understand why I was gone all day on November Saturdays, or why I fell asleep at 8:00 p.m. on Saturday night.

As a happily married man now, I totally get it. He made a good call, but I never let him believe it. So, every once in a while, I throw out a comment about his wife having awfully strong fingers to hold up a duck boat. Only a strong, long, and solid relationship can withstand ridicule and downright dishonesty. But Marvin and I have shared that for more than fifty-five years. He knows me. I know him. A shooter in military school, he's as safe with a firearm as anybody I know. A few excursions over the years with some nimrods that were not, always made me appreciate that even more. Marvin knows where I am across a hedgerow without asking or seeing me. He knows when I need help, what I'm thinking and the story I'm getting ready to tell—even before I tell it. Shoot, we can talk without talking; we have that much history.

Marvin was the second person I called the morning my mother died, and he was there in five hours, living half a state away. Contrary to my ribbing about one Thanksgiving morning and the number of empty unsuccessful 16-gauge hulls he shucked while a lottery-winning covey flew up and down a hedgerow ahead of him and my perplexed dog, he is a good shot and an even finer fellow. The duck cuppings have been quicker, the setter points stiffer, the bean fields more amber, the sun brighter, and the days afield we shared more enjoyable because he was there. No need to go on; he knows it, I know it, and the woods and fields know it—and that's enough.

There must have been something in the water in Miss Kitty's

kindergarten class, because sitting there next to me laughing at Marvin's struggle with the big shoe that day was another good friend, Richard. When we were young, Richard spent many days and nights at my house, playing, exploring, eating dinner at Grandmamma's house, trying Granddaddy's turtle soup, building forts, playing Army, and building tunnels in the spoil from newly dug ditches. We go way back.

Like most of us, Richard grew up hunting and fishing. Both he and his father were in our local "Dove Hunters Society," a group consisting of boys from ten years old to men in their seventies. Winter dove hunting was our specialty, and, during Christmas break, we would hunt almost every day. You don't see that much anymore; too many video games I suppose.

After high school, I did not see Richard much. Still, we always kept in touch and would periodically see each other at home in the dove fields.

When we were in our thirties, he moved back home and took a traveling sales position which frequently brought him my way toward the Outer Banks. He'd stay with me while he was in town and pretty soon, we made plans to quail hunt together each weekend during the season. Both of us were single then and though it didn't seem like it at the time, we had hours to burn. When you have a long history together dating back to the age of five, it only takes a little dust-brushing to get set up again.

Richard and I hunted together for several years in our thirties until the quail population waned and he and I both got married and had children. But if there were still wild birds, we would both be out there walking the fields. As the wild birds and perhaps some of the testosterone-driven bloodlust began to decline, we sometimes manufactured excuses to bypass some of the usual haunts and head to the new Hardees to sample one of their new Monster Burgers. If we were feeling particularly lazy after the debauchery at Hardees, we convinced ourselves it just might possibly still be too early to hunt the afternoon coveys, and that we needed to support the new Dairy Queen. The county was progressing, and we had fewer birds because of it. But there were more places to gorge, and our metabolisms could still take it back then, so all was not bad. Even as the bird counts dropped, Richard and I had many productive days. One in particular stands out. On a February day, while we were walking around a huge cutover through standing beans, one of the dogs ventured away from the wooded edge and cat-walked down a ditch bank well out into the field. As Richard and I looked on with both pragmatic skepticism and boyish hopefulness, the dog slammed into a point, fifty yards from the cutover. Richard will tell you that his dad's dog did some pretty work and found them first. He's right, to some extent. I can assure you his dog did do some pretty backing to my man in charge, Mack. Regardless of which dog found them, all three dogs locked up, well away from the nearest cover. The new days of clean farming had recently taken over and that was a rarity. We took four on the rise, then proceeded to pursue the singles out into the wide-open bean field. This was not uncommon in the '60s when our dads were hunting, but in the '90s, it was more likely for us to be skunked. We crisscrossed that field watching our dogs pointing and backing, backing and pointing, flushing single after single and filling our game bags.

"ESPN," Richard called it. "This is like ESPN!" To this day, we refer to it as the ESPN hunt and we look fondly at the pictures of us kneeling there—we, in our prime, our dogs smiling, and game straps loaded with quail draped around our necks. I've duck hunted and dove hunted with Richard, but I always consider him a quail'n partner. He was there when Mom passed, too.

Like all partners, Richard is much more than a hunting comrade. He and his wife Christie stood with my wife, Susan, and me in our yard one afternoon when we were trying to have a child and the odds were not necessarily in our favor. "Can we pray for you?" was Richard's question. He and I had known each other for forty years but I did not recall ever praying for him or vice versa. All four of us held hands and prayed right there in the broad daylight in our yard.

A little over a year later, our beautiful daughter was born. My wife and I have returned the favor several times, praying for Richard and his family. I'm not sure our prayers were anywhere near as effective, but they were sincere, heartfelt, and faithful. Once you have seen prayer work and experienced a new baby come into this world because of it, you want to reciprocate. Seeing Richard, a long-time friend with a similar background, become so dedicated to a more faithful life encouraged me to seek out my own journey. My life has been much more fulfilling because of it. For that and for many enjoyable fall afternoons chasing birds and pointed tails, I owe him much.

∙ ∙ ∙

I met Herb later in life by answering an ad for a puppy. He sold me that yellow Lab, Luke, and afterwards we became good friends and hunted together often. Herb was mostly my duck'n partner and we spent many mornings in the swamps and marshes of eastern North Carolina.

One particular hunt is referred to as the "tether pole" hunt. The water was way up on the Roanoke floodplain that winter and we found some ducks using on a submerged logging road next to some big timber. That morning in the dark, we drove around flooded timber and finally reached a point where the road was impassable. Then we loaded the dogs, decoys and gear into the canoe and waded 500 yards to get to our agreed-upon set-up point, a huge 100-year-old oak tree that stood just off the road. It was surrounded by water on all sides, and its dropped acorns huddled close at its base like wildebeests waiting to cross the Zambezi. The water was two feet deep on the road but became rapidly deeper as it dropped off into the flooded tupelos and cypress trees. There might as well have been a spotlight on top of that tree sending out duck Morse code for "come over here!" In the pre-dawn darkness, we set up mallard decoys around the base of the tree and ringer decoys farther up the road. I hunkered down with Luke under the oak tree and got the jerk rig going, while Herb got his calls warmed up and settled next to a bush just off the road. After the grayness came, it didn't take long for the mallards to start cackling. They were not very raucous that morning, so Herb blew softly. The decoys and jerk string were working well, and we had the "illusion set," as Herb called it. I don't think we saw more than 200 birds that day, but every flock looked at us and liked us. They would bank over the tree, necks outstretched and swiveling as they inspected the landing site, cut some air, then bank again. Herb and I like to shoot 'em in the nose, feet down and "breastesies up," as we say, so he kept letting them circle... and circle... and circle—even if they were just fifteen yards in the air.

The first flock of the day just about lit on Luke's nose, but Herb let them pass one more time just to get them sitting at the right angle. I swear he did it as much to cut an eye at my reaction as he did to lure the ducks in closer. We both knew they were done, and he got his reaction.

"Ummph," I mumbled, beneath my facemask, which Herb knew meant "Geez, if they circle one more time, they're gonna take it on the chin." And they did.

We watched and waited on four flocks that morning, each one banking, dipping, and circling that oak tree on a rope. We finished the day taking pictures with the dogs in the canoe, a limit of greenies strapped over the side and the "Tether Pole Tree" in the background. The numbered deer stand sign that was hanging on that tree is now displayed in my hunting camp, alongside a picture of me and the dogs and one of the hulls I found a year later while working on the road before deer season. Unlike the memory, that Remington Steel number 3 is rusted up a little. But like the memory, it is a representation of what a hunt can be.

We had our share of frustrating days, too. One such day, we

paddled out to a blind in the middle of a flooded cutover. We sat there for a few hours and saw no ducks, so Herb decided to paddle over into some willows to scout for feathers. About twenty minutes later, I heard all sorts of aluminum smashing and oars banging and a few words I should not put into print. I could tell he was still alive by the array of colorful language bombarding the swamp, but I knew something had happened and decided it was probably a dipping. I sat there, popped some Rolos and debated how I would walk the line between acting concerned and willfully being a smart aleck when he returned. A few minutes later, I saw him paddling toward the blind, looking like a nutria that had not preened in a while.

"You ain't going to believe this!" he said. "A branch went right down the barrel and flipped my gun out of the canoe. Of course, I reached for it, and here I went—right over the side."

"You ok?" I asked, half chuckling, half concerned no duck would venture here now.

"Heck yeah, but I'm wet." He crawled into the blind, shed his waders, removed his jacket, rolled up his pants, and hopped up on the edge of the blind in the sixty-degree weather. We drank Sundrop and ate Rolos.

"What are the odds of a branch going right down a barrel when you're canoeing?" he kept muttering between Rolos.

"About the same as us killing anything with all the racket you caused. I imagine some of 'em hit the road back to Canada, probably thinking an aluminum plant was opening up round here," I offered.

But what goes around comes around. In just two years, I took my own dip as the other paddler in the round bottom death trap I was captaining reached for a dead duck. I couldn't even get "Don't!" out of my mouth before I was hearing everyone laugh—through the water. Funny how sound carries through swamp water. Luckily, it was only waist deep. As we headed out, soaked gear and waterlogged egos loading down the canoe to the gunwales, a wayward Coast Guard helicopter picked that very moment to fly low right over us. How in the world, out of all the coastline needing protection in North Carolina, that helicopter picked that very instant to inexplicably fly 100 miles inland over the middle of a flooded bottomland is a pure mystery.

"There they are Bill. You can quit hollering! They'll get you with that drop basket!" came the start. Even Herb's son joined in. You would think I would have gotten some sort of empathy, if not sympathy. Nope, not happening. Cleaned my gun for hours that night.

Herb later made the mistake of introducing me to turkey hunting and to the absolute delight of my wife, I then developed a new passion. "Yeah!" she said, as I inventoried all of my new turkey attire after I was bitten. "Another reason the yard won't get mowed."

Like many hunters, I was tested at first and had trouble bagging that introductory Tom. One morning, an old bruiser stood cemented to a cypress branch sixty-five yards out, strutting back and forth, hammering through the swamp. But he wouldn't fly down to the ground, despite all of Herb's cutting and purring. Finally, after two and a half hours, Herb stood up and yelled at the bird, "I can't take it anymore! Go on!" I felt the same way.

On another hunt, Herb called one to within ten yards. I raised the gun, and the trigger wouldn't budge. I shucked the shell and still couldn't pull it. I had cleaned the gun after duck season and put it together wrong. We were both exasperated.

On still another morning hunt, I missed one that was angling at thirty-seven yards, and hit a sapling right in front of him that I frankly never saw. That one really got me since we were hunting at Herb's club, a revered eastern North Carolina hunt club, whose members were always extremely graceful to me and whom I respected immensely.

During that day, as expected, nobody disparaged me at all when they found out the details of the hunt. All were gracious and gentlemanly. "Don't worry about it, Bill, it happens."

"You'll get him."

We've all been there, and it helps. It doesn't heal it, but it helps. I don't know how long you wait before ribbing a man about a missed shot, but it should be the proper amount of time. Well, evidently the designated recuperation time is twelve hours.

That night, as we ate dinner with George and Leon, two long-time members older than Herb and me by twenty years, we were talking the usual politics and hunting club-type stuff. The gentlemanly atmosphere permeated and nothing at all had been said about my turkey. On the widescreen tuned to the National Geographic Channel, a herd of hippos was stampeding toward a river. As Leon walked by, he nonchalantly and without so much as glancing my way asked, "Bill, you reckon you could hit one of those?"

I looked at Herb, partly in disbelief and partly about to bust a gut. "I'm not sure, Leon, probably not today," I humbly admitted. We all laughed. It was the right bump at the right moment. Hunters know this. Leon would have been a good partner had I met him early on. Finally, after three years of trying, my day came. Herb and I were walking back to the truck at 10:30 a.m. when we heard a gobbler hammering at least a third of a mile away. Late for work, we stood there and debated whether or not to go after him.

"One thing for sure," I said, "we ain't going to kill him in the truck. Let's go get him." One of life's little decisions right there.

As we approached, we realized there were two Toms gobbling and figured one was maybe a jake. After we got set up and called, the gobblers finally walked out into the field. There were actually two shooters! They both walked out into the field, heads cocking and eyes peering, looking for the attractive lady, but very alert. On the count of three, we smoked 'em. Those two fans are on my wall now and I have never looked back.

In addition to many mornings leaned against oak trees listening for owl hoots and peering up through the canopies at the materializing first flocks, Herb and I have spent many days working on deer stands, cabins, food plots, duck holes, and game cameras. But it's not work when you're with a partner. While I can be outgoing when I need to be and as much the life of the party as the next guy, my nature is probably good ol' eastern North Carolina reserved—until I warm up to you. I would never have suspected at age forty-one, I'd meet a good friend by answering a dog ad. But I did. And we've been partners ever since.

My wife, bless her heart, was indoctrinated into this life when we met. She became a hunting partner during our first two years of marriage when we regularly duck and dove hunted together. But she had to be coaxed. The first morning I got up to go duck hunting after we were married, she woke up as I did at 3:00 a.m. and offered, "Sweetie, you want me to get up and make you eggs?"

Do what? Uh . . . say what? Like falling down on a busy street, I quickly regrouped, and looked around to make sure nobody was watching. "Baby that would be so nice. You don't have to do that," I falsely and very briefly ventured.

"Oh no, I want to," came the reply.

In forty years of hunting, I never had anyone get up and make me eggs at 3:00 a.m. I'd found a keeper!

The next week, a divorcee at work warned me that it wouldn't last. But kind of like shooting mallards on the edge of an approaching front, you've got to go with it until either the weather gets too bad, or they stop flying. It did stop after that first year and now if I so much as make a mouse noise getting out of the bed, I must carry my bitten-off head under a shot wing to get out the door.

"Get all of that gear of yours packed up so you don't wake me up," is the usual night-before directive. Of course, my comments about the absence of eggs after that first year do not help, either. While we don't hunt together much anymore, we had some memorable ones.

I can still hear Susan admonishing me when I didn't see her hit her very first duck because I was shooting mine on the other side of the blind. Imagine the audacity. Not something I've ever had from any other partner.

Another morning, I stepped onto ice at the edge of a beaver pond and promptly sliced both boot bottoms of my waders wide open. The freezing water just piled in. "I guess we'll go home now," Susan happily proclaimed, turning her headlight toward the truck, a wide grin peeking through her balaclava.

"Oh no," I informed her. "Let's see what's flying." Her reaction sent all the animals scattering like that old butter commercial when Mother Nature says it's not nice to fool her.

After three hours standing waist deep in ice cold water and only killing a few ducks, I was done. I basically fell and rolled out of the woods, miraculously not breaking my frozen ankles. I couldn't feel anything below my waist, but I knew my ears were still operable as I heard Susan's unabashed laughter echo throughout the woods, all the way to the truck.

"Let's get you home and I'll make you some hot chocolate," she offered, as I slid behind the steering wheel. She looked at me like I had a third eye when I told her we first had to drive an hour out of our way to get new waders. "Duck season still has a week left! And it's finally cold!" I educated her.

At the sporting goods store, I waited outside in my underwear—in the truck, of course—while she got my new waders. I suppose she thought she had a real jewel that day. I knew I did. Susan was a hunting partner for only a brief year or so, but she's my life partner, and I did a fine day's work when I married her.

While Susan rarely hunts with me anymore, our daughter, Sarah, has become my newest partner. When she was very young, Sarah and I spent several relaxing afternoons under old growth beeches looking for squirrels, or coloring, or just cuddling and talking, not really worrying about the game bag. We also sat in lawn chairs at the edge of ponds, Barbie pole in hand, waiting for bream to impale themselves on her hook, while we giggled and talked and played with the crickets in the bait container.

Later, we progressed to sighting in rifles while preparing to shoot her first deer and practiced shooting turkey targets, getting ready for that first gobbler.

Finally, the monumental days came when she bagged that first deer and claimed her first gobbler. We've sat together in December deer stands and scrunched up next to each other at the base of bottomland tupelos in the awakening spring turkey woods, and then fished for rock and bream those same afternoons. Just recently, she caught her first four-pound bass. We're well on our way to building our own portfolio of memories.

Before Sarah was born, I made the unwavering commitment to introduce her to the outdoors and expose her to all the grandeur, peace, and wonderment that it embodies. At first, she probably went along because it was time to be with Daddy, have fun and eat snacks—or color and maybe see a bushy tail. But over the last few years, I've seen that gleam in her eye take hold. Now she snaps her head and gets still when the owls hoot, and when that first gobbler of the morning hammers, she's immediately in the game and ready to get set. When a deer steps into the shooting lane, she's all business and even gets a bit jittery. They say if you haven't done your work by the time a child is thirteen, it won't get done. There's a lot of parenting left for Susan and me, and boys and college have come onto the scene, but I think the woods has staked out its territory, just like it did with me fifty years ago.

With your child as your partner, you have another chance to relive your youth and see in her the excitement that you once had. You can once again see that first deer, or first squirrel, or first turkey. You have the opportunity to sit under a familiar old oak and see her marvel, just like you did, at her first autumn afternoon surrounded by red and yellow leaves falling like confetti and surrendering to the settling cold front. As she matures and the grip of the woods tightens on her, you can take comfort knowing that you've done your part to ensure the reverence and passion will continue and that another has been introduced to the beauty and intricate symbioses around us. If not confidence, you certainly have a valid hope that just maybe, that old oak will see another guardian sit at its base one day. Hunting and fishing with your child is God's way of allowing you to see his blessings all over again—from perhaps a slightly different view.

There's something unique about all partners. I can usually tell within five minutes after meeting someone if I would even think of inviting them into my small fraternal cadre of like-minded devotees. When I was still in banking and brand new to one of the markets I served, I visited for the first time an elderly gentleman who had for years been one of our very best customers in the area. Mr. Herbert was retired, so I went to his home. His gracious wife greeted me at the door and led me to their den at the back of the house, where Mr. Herbert waited. "I will get us some lemonade and cookies. Is that okay with you Bill?" came her southern grace.

"Yes, Ma'am," I replied, still standing.

"Have a seat, Bill." Mr. Herbert gestured with an outstretched arm.

As I did, I thanked him for his loyalty to our company over the years. Then we discussed farming, the changes in the tobacco industry and in banking, and in his hometown—all reflections of the rapidly progressing times around us. After thirty minutes of business, I noticed some of the quail prints in the den, and we got started on bird hunting. Probably sensing the coming hours, his lovely wife politely excused herself and found something that needed her attention. Mr. Herbert, almost eighty, informed me that he had hunted the little brown gentlemen since he was a teen. We debated setters vs. pointers, remembered certain hedgerows and fields, talked about our best backing dogs, discussed staunchness vs. steadiness, and covered training, retrieving, and covey rises. I listened intently to some of his tales from over sixty years of his hunting with friends, both living and gone, and he understood my stories perhaps even better than I—although I didn't realize it at the time. I could still see the eye of a bird hunter flickering behind his glasses. For just a few hours, we were both there in the fields; he behind his dogs, and me behind my Mack, watching them quiver, listening to the tweeting birds, and preparing for the rush of the rise.

Before I knew it, it was 6:00 p.m. We'd talked for three hours, yet it had seemed like only thirty minutes. As we stood up, Mr. Herbert looked me in the eye, stuck out his hand and with a firm handshake, said, "Bill, I wish I'd met you thirty years ago. I would have loved to have hunted with you."

Well, that kind of threw me. That's about as good a compliment as a man can get in my opinion, and I had felt the same way about him. "I do too, Mr. Herbert. It would have been a real pleasure," I responded, firmly pressing my hand into his and looking back into the eye of a man who wished he could still get out in it and enjoy the whipping tails.

Walking to my truck, I reaffirmed to myself my dedication to make sure time was set aside to enjoy what someday I would be too old to do.

A year later, I stood outside Mr. Herbert's church with the rest of the overflow crowd. I couldn't hear a word of the funeral service, but it didn't matter. He would have been my partner, and that is what you do.

I think the natural tendency as you get older is to envision everything through the veil of how we think we remember it used to be. Nothing today, we pronounce, is like it was when our youthful minds were impressionable and malleable. I suppose our parents thought the same, and likewise, their parents. Surely, my granddaddy thought my long hair at fifteen was an abomination, and he was probably right. "The children now love luxury. They have bad manners, contempt for authority; they show disrespect for elders and love chatter in place of exercise," wrote Socrates. Sound familiar? Though I sometimes jokingly say to Susan, I'm a 1950s man stuck in the 2000s, or a dinosaur looking over my shoulder for the meteor, I have in fact always looked ahead. *What's the next project? What can I learn next?* But I also have a strong need to look back and reminisce about good times in the past. Sure, I conveniently downplay the days spent standing in beaver ponds with duckless air above; long afternoons walking through muddy fields weighted down by wet and cold briar-faced pants; frigid days on the Sound endured by stomping frozen feet in duck blinds, and those frustrating gobblers I messed up before I bagged one. Yet, I have a hard time actually thinking of any miserable days afield . . . because there were none. Instead, there has been a lifetime of memories, absolute unmatched natural beauty, and honest, genuine sport groomed by the serenity of the outdoors and nurtured by lifelong friends and close family. Knowing the precariousness involved in any of it actually happening can be humbling. If I hadn't attended kindergarten here, or played football there, or answered an ad there, or gone on a blind date here, or met a friend while attending to his banking needs, or prayed for a daughter in a yard one afternoon with a close partner, all of these memories—my life—may not have happened. Knowing how life can take such quirky blind turns leading to long straight stretches of glorious thoroughfares gives me the desire to keep trying new things—to relinquish, maybe just a little, the middle-aged grip on what is perceived to have been better back in the day, and accept inevitable change. After all, in nature's rhythm, summer trees do release their leaves in the fall wind, with full expectations of the next spring. Things do change. Quail decline. The pre-dawn march through the swamp gets harder. The winter doves seem to get quicker and mornings in blinds grow colder. But at the same time, our rich recollections of days afield with partners allow us to be there again—right in the thick of it. Whether you do it through memories with long-time friends, or by sitting with a young man in your den one day talking about your vibrant years, or by laughing at your daughter jumping up and down beside her first turkey, you can always go back. Partners know this.

The River Road

Nowadays, my hectic schedule is filled with work, honey-dos and attending my teenage daughter's performances while trying to keep some semblance of friendships—all despite my natural tendency to be a hermit. Converse to the texts, tweets, computer searches, ringtones and spreadsheets of today, the days of my childhood in the 1960s moved at a much slower pace. Many homes in our rural area were still heated by pot-belly stoves in the winter and enjoyed no air conditioning in the summer. We did not get air conditioning until 1968, and my grandfather never had it installed. Hot summer days could be rather unexciting for a boy. But I never moped around proclaiming, "I'm bored," because I knew if I didn't find something to do, Mom would find it for me; and my something-to-do was always better than her something-to-do. You didn't say you were bored in 1967. Otherwise, the garden got hoed, the yard got mowed or the store got swept. You didn't go there. Nope. Yet adults, lost in their bustling bee-like world of get-it-done now, don't understand there will always be something that has to be done, and therefore it can wait. Kids, on the other hand, do not comprehend the seemingly hollow exploits of parents trying to keep their striving noses just ahead of Mr. and Mrs. Jones, thus missing some of life's minute windows that allow the real panorama of this world to shine through.

Although unhindered by the corruption of maturation, a child is regrettably stunted by his or her inability to always think of productive things to do. But the innate desire to have fun can also catapult a willing child from an otherwise obscure afternoon into a few hours that make a memory for a lifetime. An adult's role is to observe, listen, and notice when one of those brief windows opens. If both do what they are supposed to do, we'll be the better for it, and life can happen. A window opened for me one summer day in 1967. Mom put away her daily stresses and she and I shared an afternoon . . . so fleeting in my childhood.

As I sat in the double rocker, grinding rhythmically against the grit on the concrete floor of our country store, the fog from my Granddaddy's unfiltered camels hung heavy in the air. He was pacing back and forth between the red tin Coca-Cola drink box and the wide-open double doors at the front of our store. In

Granddaddy's left hand, the omnipresent Camel was trapped delicately between his brown-stained thumb and index finger, while his right hand strategically held at the ready a murderous flyswatter. My daughter probably doesn't even know what a flyswatter is, but in '67 that lethal four-inch square piece of plastic at the end of the metal loop could be the ultimate, sudden, horrific—and entertaining to a boy—splattering demise of a naive fly anywhere inside the store. As far as I'd seen in my brief seven years, Granddaddy Fentress was a man of few words. But even the pea-brained insect population was smart enough to stay away from his lethal ambling combination of smoke, puffing, coughing, relentless pursuit and accurate swinging that made Ted Williams look like a little leaguer.

Granddaddy had been shot by a German soldier in WWI. A mere fly was certainly not going to get the best of him. This was pre-air conditioning August in eastern North Carolina and the walk-in customers we typically serviced were scarcer than a Republican county commissioner that day. As I slouched in the old double-seater rocking chair, matching my rhythm to Granddaddy's pacing, and trying to decide whether it would be more fun to be Mickey Mantle and hit rocks out of the parking lot with a stick, or to climb the sycamores outside, Mom intuitively asked if I would like to ride down to the river to go fishing and swimming. Well, there you go! That, my friend, is a window. I hopped immediately out of the rocker, yelling, "Yes, Ma'am!" over my shoulder, as I ran to our house next door to get my swimsuit. Upon my return, Mom gathered the cane poles out of the corner of the store next to the kerosene pump and I grabbed a pound of frozen shrimp from the meat case. Unlatching the tailgate on the light blue '66 Chevy pickup, Mom loaded all of it into the bed as I hopped onto the scorching hot vinyl bench seat, quickly shoving my hands underneath me while shifting my scalded legs back and forth like somebody trying to clog sitting down. I can't even remember the last time I saw anyone sit on their hands in a truck—or if anyone still does—or if anyone still needs to? I waved goodbye to Granddaddy, and he waved back, peering at us over his wire frame L.B.J. glasses, undoubtedly more concerned about the corn and beans growing in the field and where prices would be in the fall, than the delights the cool river water could give a child. Nonetheless, there was a glint in his eye, as he stooped there waving. I guess the river, forever a slave to the daily tides, never loses its own gentle tugging. Our truck was relatively new, having just replaced the red International pickup Daddy had bought for the farm years earlier. It smelled of dust, greasy farm parts and hot vinyl, but having spent the majority of my years riding around the fields with Mom, I was as comfortable in that cab as a hound lying in the sun on a fall day. To get to the river road, we had to first drive a mile on a roughly paved two-lane black top; it was the kind of asphalt country road that a seven-year-old boy stumped his big toe on at least three times every summer, painfully peeling back the top layer of skin every time. I hung my head out the truck window the entire way, feeling the welcome cool breeze against my face, looking at the fields and willfully antagonizing a couple of dogs chasing us. Back then, there was little traffic for them to worry about, nor to interrupt a boy's enjoyment of a pickup ride. As we turned right onto the river road, the half-mile tree-lined single-lane dirt and gravel path that took us to Bay River, an excited anticipation flowed up in me, pumped by years of summer afternoon fun at this place. Whether we were going swimming, fishing, or just planning to spend time on the pier, I always got that summertime Christmassy feeling when we turned onto the river road.

Mom asked if I would help her unlock the chain gate, so I leaped out of the passenger side as fast as I could. As she held the rusted chain tight, I put the key in the lock and turned it. Then she let the chain clang though the iron post until it hit the ground with a familiar metallic thud that meant we were on our way. I slid back into the truck through her side and sat there on the sticky bench seat as Mom got behind the wheel and put the truck in drive. *Here we go!* I thought.

At the beginning of our journey and to our left there were tremendous old-growth pine trees. Those trees must have been seventy-five years old; they almost entirely shaded the road, giving the first few hundred yards a cathedral-like setting. The trees also provided the road with a permanent coating of pine straw that cushioned the sound of the mud-grip farm tires against the gravel. The hissing drone of summer locusts seemed to emanate from all corners of the surrounding forest, and I could only guess at how many thousands of huge translucent brown skeletons those big beetles were leaving attached to the pine bark. A squirrel bolted from the left, intent on getting to a stand of small maples on the right side of the road. But he changed his mind in mid-scamper, looked at us, zig-zagged, and then decided the safety of the big pines was his best bet. Giggling, I glanced up at Mom. She winked at me and chuckled.

The sun poked through tiny breaks in the pine canopy and as we silently rolled down the path, it intermittently speckled the light blue hood of the truck with a constantly changing array of shadowy designs. To the right of the road was an old field, where we had once raised hogs but where now only stood a seven-acre patch of fescue. At the back of that field and just before the first curve of the road to the right, there were two old barns where we had kept corn for those hogs. I remembered how just two years earlier, when I was a little boy of five, Mom made me stay in the truck as she fed corn to the hogs out of a bushel basket filled from the barn. There was an old boar in that field that was, at the very least, unpredictable and she did not want me anywhere near him. Beyond the barns, the river road veered gradually to the right. The tall pines at the entrance transitioned into younger and smaller pine trees on the left of the path, but on the right side the old hog pen changed into a mature hardwood ridge dominated by three huge mature beech trees. The ridge dropped off to a swamp on the far side, where water usually stood among several decaying gum trees, live gums, and some poplars. Every once in a while, driving past that ridge, we would see a deer browsing, a squirrel scurrying among the beeches, or a pileated woodpecker flying down to the flooded gum trees to hopefully hammer out a tune that you could hear for a half mile. But that day, I saw nothing as I stared through the open window and squirmed in my seat to get a better look at the swampy area. The river was just a couple of turns ahead.

After we passed the beech ridge, the road curved back to the left and transitioned into a mixed stand of twenty-year-old pines and hardwoods on both sides. This area always had low-hanging branches that scraped against the truck; it was imperative that a curious boy intent on peering into the woods to spot any possible sign of animals, keep his head and hands inside the window so as not to get slapped by one of nature's switches. One of those branches was just making its grinding pass by my side of the truck and I was giving it its proper respect, when Mom suddenly stopped the truck. "Well look at that!" she admiringly exclaimed, as she stared through the sun-splotched windshield.

"What Momma?" I asked, as I spun toward her.

"Right there in the road. Do you see those quail? And there . . . there . . . look at those babies!" She encouraged me to look quickly.

I sat up on the seat and there, not fifteen feet in front of the truck, marched two adult quail and eight chicks. The momma and daddy quail were unabashedly leading the chicks across the road in a respectful but unhurried manner, as if thanking Momma for stopping. Yet, at the same time, they seemed to be proclaiming in no uncertain terms that they had the right-of-way. The little chicks were cranking their tiny legs just as fast as they could, oblivious to the truck, Mom, me, or anything but their parents. I looked over at Mom, but she never said a word; she just kept staring at the quail. We sat there in silence for a couple of minutes until the whole entourage made it into the woods. When they had cleared the road, I looked back at Mom. She still sat there staring at the road.

"Look!" she said. "Billy, do you see that momma quail?"

I looked back at the road and the momma quail had marched back out to the center of the path. There, she started spinning, flailing, flapping and generally causing a big ruckus.

"What's wrong? Is she hurt?" I shouted.

"No, she's pretending to be hurt so we won't bother her baby chicks," Mom replied. Then she turned and, as a warm smile spread across her face, added, "She's their mother. It's her job to protect them. She's fine. I promise," she assured me.

After a minute or two, the hen quail stood up straight, flapped a couple of times and walked defiantly off the road to join her family.

Mom slowly drove the truck forward. As we passed the spot where the covey entered the woods, I strained to catch a glimpse of them as they squiggled off into the underbrush, as if playing an avian game of follow-the-leader. I turned back toward Mom, fully expecting her to tell me more about the quail. Instead, she shifted to second and kept driving.

We jostled down the last eighth of a mile of the river road in silence. I kept glancing over at Mom, but she didn't say anything. As we pulled into the yard of the cabin where the road ended, Mom cut off the truck. As tradition and respect for this place necessitated, we both took in the view for a moment. The river sprawled out wide and glass-calm in front of us. Beyond the drop-off, local trawlers puttered left and right, their diesels breaking the stillness with a monotone hum, their nets trailing behind them and probing the brackish water for shrimp to take to the docks in Vandemere and Hobucken. A jumping mullet catapulted itself out of the water, spread its gills wide—as if gulping for the humid air—then belly-flopped, briefly interrupting the serene order. A seagull plunged beak-first into the water, proudly surfacing with a fatback in its mouth. Other seagulls chimed in with their mocking laughter, taunting their skilled partner. On our left, the subtle waves lapped at the shore of Chinquapin Ridge, the same ridge where my father had found arrowheads with his brothers.

I couldn't take it any longer and hastily scrambled out of the truck, sprinted down to the water, avoided the old piling on the left and jumped in. As the cool water surrounded me with its amniotic embrace, I popped up just in time to see Mom unloading the cane poles and laughing. The boys in New Bern had Middle Street and the department stores with all the toys, and the boys in Bayboro had the ball fields next to their houses, but I had Bay River—and during this time of year, there was no comparison.

The next two hours were spent by me swimming and then by both of us fishing. We didn't catch anything, but then we didn't expect to catch much during the middle of the afternoon. It wasn't meant to be just a fishing trip. It was an escape for a mother and her son. It turned out to be one of those perfect but brief afternoons, where everything is forever recorded in the mind of a seven year old. It ended around 5:00 p.m.; the window closed, though not with my approval.

...

During the next ten years, the river road was a sanctuary for me. Prior to turning sixteen, I regularly rode my bike from the store with my rusty tacklebox and a half-pound box of frozen shrimp stuffed into a galvanized bucket hanging from the handlebars. Kids these days may have the nimbleness to play two different video games simultaneously, but I bet they can't ride a banana bike while holding two rods and reels, with a bouncing bucket and tacklebox constantly whipping the front wheel right to left—with two dogs chasing you. That was about as nimble as I've ever been right there. Several dependable Zebco 202s and 33s hauled in countless croakers and trout until one day, the ultimate rig arrived from Herter's; it was a Mitchell 300, which I still own today. I never could master a bait-casting reel and even now, still occasionally get a backlash. During those boyhood years, every time I turned down that river road, I always got excited, while anticipating catching that elusive three-pound speck, a two-spot puppy-drum or just my usual half-pound croakers and bream-like pinfish. But the river road was not just a path to good fishing.

Each year as the fall approached, thoughts turned to hunting. Many times, I walked down to the river in the early pre-dawn moonlight, the old Winchester 24 broken over my shoulder, so I could be there when the bushytails first began moving. That beech ridge was my favorite spot and those three magnificent behemoths produced more than a few fantastic mornings. One frosty Thanksgiving morning, I peeled two out of the same beech, then I quietly walked the rest of the way to the river and took another as he jumped from a tall pine right at the water's edge. He fell thirty feet and made a huge tea-colored splash when he hit the tannic water. I had to wade out into the river to retrieve him but that was okay; I'd never killed three in one morning until that day.

There was also the time I spotted a squirrel high in one of the seventy-five-year-old pines on a bitter cold December morning. He was holding on gallantly during a strong thirty-mile-an-hour wind and his buffeted gray fur gave off a reddish hew as the morning sun reflected on him at just the right angle. The high-brass number 5s hit their mark and his fall was long and memorable to a boy in his second autumn of hunting.

I also remember coming home from high school one day after football season had ended my senior year. Mom greeted me in the kitchen with the news I'd been waiting to hear. "There's a letter on the dining room table. It's from Carolina." She, of course, hadn't opened it, though I knew she was anxiously anticipating their decision.

"Really?" I tried to act seventeen-year-old-boyish cool.

"Yes, I haven't opened it, Billy, but you know I wanted to." Mom stood at the kitchen sink, as I walked into the dining room and put my books on the table. There it was, with the *Old Well* stamped on the envelope.

Well, this is it, bud, I thought. I hesitated to make sure Mom wasn't standing there. Slowly, I opened it and unfolded the letter; the same letter I still have today in the cedar box on my dresser. *Congratulations William . . .* Filled with excitement, I walked back into the kitchen to see Mom turn around. Tears filled her eyes, as I nodded the decision. At seventeen, you think you know why your mother is crying, but you don't really know until you're older and have your own children.

I hugged Mom, as anti-climatically as only a seventeen-year-old boy can; I grabbed my Remington bolt-action .22, Super-X bullets, and headed to the river road. Football had cramped my squirrel hunting until now and I wanted to catch up.

The base of one of the beeches provided just the right curve to support my back and the warmth of the early November setting sun permeated the woods. The smell of crunched leaves, woody bark, browning pine needles, fallen gumballs and all of autumn's changes was thick that evening. Comfortable, thankful, and secure in my familiar surroundings, I took a deep and prideful breath. *I'm in!* I'd always wanted to go to Chapel Hill and I'd made it. Scouting toward the swamp, I saw no squirrels, so I leaned back, closed my eyes and rested. Thoughts drifted to days spent swimming and fishing and mornings stalking quietly up and down the road. Even then, I suspected that I might never feel the same in those woods once I left home for Chapel Hill the following summer. I was happy and excited, but there was a rightful mourning in the woods, and a mindful peace.

My eyes opened just before dark to see ripples on the water beneath the gum trees. I immediately recognized the sound of cut seeds splashing into the water with the familiar plip-plop that signaled only one thing: Mr. Bushytail was somewhere in the treetops. After scrutinizing each branch above the ripples, I was able to find that gentleman. Resting the rifle on the side of the beech, I studied him for a few minutes through the old Weaver. He was content, totally absorbed in his daily business of survival; I was simply a tolerated observer. The light was fading, and a red glow began to silhouette the swamp. A front was coming, the air was turning cool, and I wanted to get home to supper and maybe even give Mom more quality time. I stood up, slung the .22 over my shoulder, and walked the twenty yards to the river road. Standing there between two curves, I turned to take one last look at the squirrel as it speedily monkey-barred limb-to-limb toward the other side of the swamp, expedited by an all-knowing owl hooting deep in the timber. I stood there taking it all in; the cold air, the animal sounds, the familiarity and surety of it all, watching the sun set behind those big beeches for the last time of my youth.

The next year, while I was at school, the tall seventy-five-year-old pines and all but one of the beeches were cut down. The river road changed forever. The next four years, I spent less time hunting and fishing as college life took precedence, but I walked that road at least twice a year. It always gave me and still gives me solitude that I can only get from one other place.

Forty-three years have passed since that last squirrel hunt in November of 1977. There are now just a few tall, skinny, widely spaced pines in a cutover where the old pines once stood. The open beech ridge is gone, transformed into mediocre hardwood undergrowth. But in the middle of that mundane landscape, one of the big beeches still remains, a sentinel to the memories of a North Carolina boy's maturation. The pines where that quail family once strode is now a campground and the big pine on the edge of the river where I shot the squirrel that Thanksgiving morning has long since fallen into the water, a victim of Hurricane Dennis.

I am now a sixty-year-old man with a daughter of my own. She just got her Carolina letter, and I now understand what my mother felt as she stood in the kitchen that day. I understand the momma quail and I think I understand what Mom felt as she sat there in the farm truck, looking through the windshield. I now know why she was silent until we got to the river.

A few years ago, I helped a good friend and a few other hunting acquaintances build a couple of duck blinds in an impoundment in Florence, located on the other side of the river from my boyhood home. It was an atypical July day, comfortable with highs in the 80s. After hours of hard but rewarding work, the kind only duck hunters know, we headed home. On the way out to Highway 55, we pulled into the newly cleared driveway of a home under construction to get some water out of the back of the truck. When we pulled into the driveway, we both immediately spotted a hen and daddy quail crossing the driveway with seven or eight little chicks following in single file. My friend and I grew up quail hunting, so we both excitedly pointed them out to each other. We sat there and watched as the momma and daddy quail gallantly led the chicks into the high grass. Then, unexpectedly, the daddy came back out to ensure that we were not getting any closer. We sat there and watched until he finally decided we were not a threat and rejoined his covey. It suddenly occurred to me that we were just across Bay River and probably only three miles as a crow flies from where I'd seen the quail family with my mother.

"Sit here, I'll get the water," I told my friend. Retrieving the water from the cooler in the back of the truck, I paused for a moment to look up at the tall pines as they swayed back and forth in the July breeze. I thought back to my many experiences on the river road, the beeches, the old pines, the locusts, the quail family crossing, and Mom's warm expression. I thought about my own daughter, and I said a short prayer that she would have the chance to see quail like this, understand the strong family ties that experiences in nature can provide, and that she may hear a bobwhite whistle on our farm.

Over the last ten years and with God's grace, those prayers have been answered. Though she has not seen the number of quail I had by her age of eighteen, Sarah has observed numerous turkeys and bears that we did not have when I was young. Since she was three, we've fished for bream and rock with Barbie poles and spinning reels, and sat in dove fields, turkey woods, deer stands, and squirrel woods, enjoying our moments. As she's been willing, I've tried to keep the fleeting windows open long enough for us to breathe that rare air. She and I are still making our memories, even though she's off to Chapel Hill. But the windows will always be open. The river road may have stopped at the water's edge, but it's never ended.

Coming Around

They say that if you live long enough you will see many things change, then evolve, then morph, and finally change one more time so that you come full circle. "What goes around comes around," they say. "History repeats itself."

While I pray leisure suits never come back in style, I am a firm believer in the above pontifications. Just the other day, I was getting into the Suburban with my daughter. As I looked at her feet, visions of sixth grade hit me right in the face. There staring back at me and encasing her feet, was a pair of Chuck Taylor Converse shoes, just like the ones I wore in 1972. The only difference was the price; they're not ten dollars anymore. I suppose everything does come back around, if you wait long enough. This was readily apparent during the 2016 turkey season, when on opening day of the North Carolina Youth Season, I took my twelve-year-old daughter turkey hunting.

Sarah and I had been working hard to get her a longbeard since she went on her first hunt with me at six years old. Looking back on that first year, I probably rushed it a little as Sarah had not even handled the shotgun yet, although she had become proficient with her .22. The real purpose that day was just to get her out in nature and hopefully, if we were lucky, see a gobbler. We certainly didn't expect to have any chance to actually bag one.

After Sarah's Easter egg hunt, we made a quick decision to go that opening afternoon of youth day. Speedily loading the truck and without taking full inventory, we grabbed a hodgepodge of camo clothing, a few coloring books and snacks, Easter candy, the twenty-gauge, some camo face paint, and then hustled to the turkey woods. Yep, you guessed it; we encountered a sight that afternoon I have never seen before—or since. Four mature gobblers came from 300 yards down a logging path to within five yards of us, gobbling their respective heads off, a mere twelve inches apart.

I had no face mask and only one camo glove; Sarah was displaying her favorite pink shirt until I covered her with my camo jacket when the gobblers were at one hundred yards.

It ended with me refusing to allow Sarah to shoot for fear of killing four, or wounding three, or wounding four, etc. We let them go, watching as they marched away, still gobbling full rolls all the way back down the logging path, unsure as to what happened but knowing that something was up. It was quite a show and Sarah, justifiably disappointed, never let me forget it.

Over the next few years, we first got her used to the twenty-gauge, and then practiced with turkey targets so she would know exactly how to shoot when she finally did get that next chance. During the subsequent seasons, a few birds came close, but Daddy could not close the deal.

In 2015, we had even asked Herb to call for us at our hunting club on the Roanoke. Having studied and hunted the wily creatures for forty years, Herb is an accomplished turkey caller. I've teased him that he is the consummate southern gentleman when it comes to willingly pointing out to any neophyte where a trophy buck is hiding, and a pretty good guy when it comes to telling his friends where a dose of ducks is using—but he is an outright liar when it comes to telling his longtime buddies or even relatives where an ol' Tom is lurking. Turkeys are his passion, and to prove it, he has impressive hooks on a leather strap that he caresses before opening day each season. "It's for mojo," he declares each year. I think he conjures up incantations with that thing, and he can make a mouth call sing. It was fitting that the first time I met Herb, he was sitting under an oak tree in his yard, his seven-year-old son nestled in his lap, aiming a twenty-gauge at a turkey target. Pulling up the driveway, I stopped the truck and watched as the boy peppered the target with Herb encouraging him. Then he stood up, hugged the boy, and walked over so we could discuss the yellow Lab puppy he'd advertised. That first contact, between a full-time quail hunter/part-time duck hunter and a full-time duck hunter/full-time turkey hunter, brought together over an ad in the newspaper, resulted in a long friendship bolstered by early mornings in duck swamps with my new dog, Luke, and Luke's mom, Lucy. The friendship was later seasoned watching Herb's son develop as a hunter and grow into a fine young man.

Now we were bringing my daughter along the same path, albeit at times hunting took a back seat to her singing engagements, plays, and a pre-teen girl's social calendar. But even today, she still wants to hunt and fish with her daddy, and with "Uncle Herbie," as she calls him. Luke has since passed, but the friendship has endured, and when I asked Herb to call for Sarah again, he was more than happy to do so—and excited to oblige.

Because rain was forecast for the opening morning of youth day, we decided to hit the woods after the weather cleared. Sarah and I left our house at noon, heading out on the two-hour drive to the hunt club. As we drove off, Susan waved and wished us luck. She knew how important this day was to me; a father wanting to see his daughter experience some of the same joys he had experienced; and to her daughter, who had worked so hard for a turkey and who enjoyed spending treasured time with her daddy.

Sarah sat next to me in the old truck, decked out in her Cabela's sweatshirt, camo pants, new boots and camo hat with her ponytail bouncing through the hole in the back. During the ride, we talked about school, boys—or knuckleheads, as I call them whenever she's within earshot—and the new play for which she was auditioning.

Later, after we hit McDonald's, the conversation turned toward the hunt. "Daddy, I really want to get one," she implored.

"I do too Sarah. You're ready. You've worked hard to get ready. You just have to be patient. Listen to me, hunting is long periods of waiting in anticipation, followed by brief but exciting seconds of pure adrenaline. Once you experience that a few times, you'll realize it. Remember shooting your first deer a couple of years ago? All of a sudden, it was there, and you got him, because you were ready. Be patient and it will happen. But you've got to be ready when the time comes. It can happen real quick."

"Okay, Daddy."

I knew she could do it. I just hoped she'd get the chance. After reaching the low ground woods and greeting Herb upon his arrival, Sarah and I were eager to start hunting, especially since the sky was clearing fast. We first tried a small food plot about a quarter mile from the cabin. Peaking around a corner in the path, we spied a gobbler with some hens and quickly got set up. Herb called while Sarah and I waited, but the Tom wouldn't come. Eventually, he trotted out of the plot and into the bottom. Sarah was disappointed, so I asked her to remember what we had discussed on the way down. "Be patient sweetie," I encouraged.

"Okay, Daddy," she agreed.

With an empty field in front us and knowing there were undisturbed birds in other parts of the property, we chose to head down another road, calling as we walked. Herb led the way while periodically hitting the box call. Unexpectedly, a gobbler popped out into the road and busted us.

"Daggone it," I said, as Sarah and Herb both threw up their hands in exasperation. Sarah was getting a little ticked, so I leaned down and told her the afternoon was young, encouraging her to hang in there.

"Bill, let's go to the field behind the cabin and sit there and call. There've been some birds using over there," Herb suggested.

"Yeah, that sounds good. Sarah, you up for that?"

"Yes, Daddy."

We cut through the woods to the field behind the cabin and, after surveying the hunting area, Sarah and I set up under a big pine tree with me seated close by her right side, and Herb calling back over our left shoulder. We positioned a hen decoy and a strutter in the field just in front of us, got the shotgun strapped to the bipod and settled in. Herb let everything calm down for about ten minutes before he hit the box call a few times. Then we sat back and waited. It had become a pleasant sunny spring afternoon with the first shadows beginning to stretch across the back of the field, gradually encasing the long hedgerow that extended away from us toward the cabin in the far distance. It was approaching turkey go-time.

In November of the previous fall, just ten yards from where we sat now, a shooter buck with a wide six-point rack had hesitated at the far side of that hedgerow, looking directly at me, and refusing to come within range of my bow. That same day, a non-shooter eight pointer, his taut shoulders filled with the fall rut and his fiery eyes inspecting each and every movement around him, had stopped chasing a doe very near where we were seated. I'd watched as he high-stepped away, neither one of us fulfilled, but both pleased with the moment. "Keep your eyes open and movement to a minimum. It can happen any time so keep your game face on, okay?" I whispered.

"Okay, Daddy, I will." As she looked up at me with her blue eyes full of anticipation, I added some last-minute face paint to her soft cheeks, hugged her and told her to be ready, alert and to "get her mess right"—which had always been my little saying to her. Herb began to intersperse some mouth clucks and purrs with rich sounding yelps from his prize box call. We'd been sitting there roughly thirty minutes when I spotted movement and slowly turned my head to the left. Herb had already seen the lone hen methodically edging toward the decoy, pecking the ground and neck-jerking her way carefully toward her perceived rival.

"Sarah," I whispered, "look, there's a hen to the left. Turn very slowly." As she did, she spotted the hen and watched as she cautiously approached the decoy. "Daddy where's the gobbler?"

"I don't know, Sarah, maybe one will come. Keep your eyes open. Shhhh."

The hen walked to within ten yards of us and camped out, pecking the ground but keeping an alert eye on her surroundings. We watched her eat, study our decoys and nervously periscope the area until I noticed movement about seventy-five yards from us, next to the hedgerow and further out in the field. Slowly, a gobbler walked out into the field. I couldn't see a beard through the tall grass and, my first thought was that an early jake had decided to come inspect the hen call before ol' boss Tom could respond. Then I spotted more movement behind him, and another gobbler walked out. Checking the hen first, I carefully raised the binoculars as the first gobbler lowered his head to the ground. *Bingo! One mature gobbler!* Then the other bird turned side to me in the afternoon sun, and there swinging below his iridescent chest, was his paintbrush. "Sarah," I whispered as I leaned over to my little girl, "there are two gobblers out there and they're both shooters."

"Daddy!" she stopped short, as her chest began to immediately heave, and her breathing became audible.

So, help me, I thought she was going to hyperventilate right there with gobblers at seventy yards and a hen at ten yards. I was thrilled, too—for her, for me, for Herb, and for the possibilities the moment presented. But we had to close the deal. "Sarah, be real still and get your game face on. I think they'll come but you've got to be still. Keep an eye on that hen." Quickly, I summarized the scene in my head. I couldn't look at Herb because he was behind us, and I knew the hen would bust us. Shoot, all this talking was more than enough in itself to cause her to be nervous. She scooted closer to the hedgerow and further from us, no doubt hearing something but unsure what it was. Thank goodness for youth day and thank goodness for our years of hunting partnership. The hen, new to this game and unrattled by hunting pressure, settled down and without looking, I knew Herb had an understanding of the turkey situation and that he likewise knew I was working to get us set. We just had to get ready. But first, I had to move the shotgun and bipod to the right so that Sarah could shoot one of the gobblers when they came within range. "Sarah, I need to move the gun. Just sit still and I will take care of it. When I move it, help me if you can."

Not the most limber guy in the world, this would take some doing. I reached around and behind to the right, grabbed the pine tree backhanded, then leaned way over and reached in front of Sarah with my left—all the while keeping an eye on the hen, still at ten yards, and the gobblers, now at sixty-five yards. When they all had their heads down, we moved the gun. It could not have worked better with grease.

"Okay Sarah, get ready. I think they'll come. When they get around that pine, you've got the green light. Enjoy watching them but get your head on right and we'll kill him."

"Daddy, I'm nervous!"

"Sarah, you can do this. We've worked on it. You're a good shot. Just do it, no problem." I had to reassure her, but wrestled whispering encouraging words vs. the inevitable outcome of the hen getting spooked.

She'd look up every once in a while, but thankfully did not put two and two together and continued her feeding while Herb serenaded her. The gobblers at sixty-five yards turned into approaching birds at fifty, and then they saw the strutting decoy.

"Get ready, Sarah, they're coming."

"Daddy!"

They covered forty yards in twenty seconds. All that was left was coming around the pine tree into the kill zone.

"Sarah, when they come around that tree, shoot the one closest."

"Daddy, I'm scared!"

Goodness, I thought, *if we mess this up, I'll never hear the end of it.*

Herb was purring and soft clucking with his mouth call, and it was a good thing because I couldn't have purred, talked to Sarah, moved the shotgun, and got it all situated by myself. "Sarah, when they go behind that tree get your left hand on the forend tight, squeeze it to your shoulder . . . line it up, then pull the trigger when the first one comes around the tree."

"Daddy, I feel like I'm going to throw up!" Her breathing was pounding and the "C" on the Cabela's logo on her shirt looked like the heart of the Grinch in that Christmas cartoon when it grows ever so many sizes too big. She was breathing so heavily that I swore the hen heard it because it was obvious that she was getting wise to these goings-on.

"Sarah, you can do it."

"Daddy, I'm nervous!"

"Sarah, are they behind that tree now from where you are sitting?"

"Yes, Daddy." Just then, she reached for the forend and got the stock nestled tight against her shoulder, just like we'd practiced so many times. Both gobblers were now in full view at ten yards—necks stretched, heads cocked—and I was sure they were getting ready to reverberate that sound that we all hate to hear; the dreaded putt. But Herb soft-purred with his mouth call and they visibly relaxed.

"Daddy, I think I'm going to throw up!"

Not exactly what a father wants to hear again when there are two shooters at ten yards, and a hunting buddy is purring his heart out, no doubt wondering what was going on and building up an artillery of wisecracks to remind his hunting partner of this failure in the future. I would undoubtedly get unmerciful grief for letting two birds escape that Herb had so skillfully called into an overly vocal dad and his daughter (of course he would only unleash that unfettered barrage on me, and not on Sarah).

"Sarah, shoot the dang bird!" I whispered.

Sarah had always been the type of girl that responded to a little pressure. I'd seen it whenever she got up and sang in front of our church or performed in plays in front of hundreds. She had even recently sung the national anthem in front of her school. We'd missed opportunities before and I knew she would be devastated if we didn't close the deal on one of these gobblers, especially with two at ten yards. And one of those big boys was wising up fast and moving away, followed closely by his less astute bud. So right then and there, I made a daddy decision; I pressed her.

She was breathing hard, chest pounding and eyes tearing a little, but I'd seen that same determination in her before, willing its way onto the scene. She hugged that buttstock tight to her shoulder, squeezed the forend even tighter and defiantly whispered, "Okay!" Basically, she was telling me she had it—and be quiet.

The next five seconds seemed like an eternity, as Herb deftly manufactured velvety purrs with his mouth call and the gobblers hung there in purgatory focusing on the live hen and the decoys. One of them knew something was up and was slinking off, but the other had returned from his brief foray toward the hedgerow. The hen had decided the hedgerow was better than listening to what must have sounded to her like a frat party, but the closest Tom could not stand the site of the hen decoy being courted by the strutter nor the purring and soft clucks from Herb. He remained.

Sarah drew a bead on him, with her cheek pressed tight on the stock and her knuckles white against the forend. There we were, after six years of work and anticipation, hours of getting her used to twenty-gauge recoil, afternoons practicing with turkey-head targets, many mornings of scouting early birds, several experiences calling in gobblers and not being able to close the last fifty yards, at least one morning lining up Herb to call for us only to have the screwgies put on us—and this was it! That is the moment we all live for right there; those last few keen seconds of anticipation that make the sport the passion that it is. There is nowhere on this planet I would have rather been than nestled close beside Sarah, under that pine tree, seeing her reaching down for that calmness—watching her grow, witnessing it all unfold. All she had to do was face her nervousness and pull the trigger. And just at that moment: Boom! The gobbler was catapulted up in the air, his head slamming backwards immediately followed by his backside. He lay sprawled out, flopping on the ground, doing the backstroke but going nowhere, his destiny as my daughter's trophy fulfilled.

No words can describe the flood of joy I felt right then. I grabbed Sarah's gun, automatically checked the safety, sprang up and started running toward the flapping gobbler. He was dead and I knew it. I'd never in my life run to a flailing bird like some of the over-reactive dudes on TV; I never saw the need to do such an idiotic thing, not me. But six years of work and my daughter's happiness—almost as much as mine—were riding on getting this bird. As I ran, I saw Herb on my left, a forty-year turkey hunter, passing me. We weren't going to let Sarah's bird get away, even if it meant these two old guys had to run him down. But no need . . . Sarah's gobbler was laid out like Thanksgiving dinner. "Sarah, you dusted him!" I yelled back at her.

"Daddy!" came the squeal only a twelve-year-old girl can emanate. "I can't believe it!" she screamed, as she ran to us. She wrapped her arms around me and gave me a great big hug. I'm telling you, it was all I could do not to break down right there. If you've ever had a daughter or son kill that first turkey, or first anything, after years of work, you know what I mean. After our long hug, she ran to Herb.

"Uncle Herbie, we got him! We got him!"

Herb was thrilled too, standing there victoriously grinning like a possum with a call hanging out of the side of his mouth. "Congratulations, Sarah! Great job! Sarah, what in the world were you and your daddy doing over there?" Herb asked.

"I thought I was going to throw up!" she shouted.

"What?"

"I thought I was going to throw up. I was soooo nervous!"

Herb laughed. "I thought I was going to shoot both you and your dad if somebody didn't pull a trigger. I didn't know what was going on, except I thought y'all were having a conversation with the turkeys or something," came the first of the wise cracks, as Herb winked over at me.

"She was nervous, and I told her to shoot the dang bird, or we would get a cussing!" I winked back.

Sarah hugged Herb tight. And I thanked him.

"I was purring, soft calling, everything I could think of to keep 'em in the game. I've never worked so hard on a turkey in my life. I didn't know what else to do!"

For a second, Herb almost reached the same octave as Sarah, but he regrouped when he sensed his high-pitched oratory could possibly be relived over future dinners.

"You did great, Herbie. Thanks buddy," I confirmed, shaking his hand. It was a solid handshake that was more than a handshake. It was measured and confirmed through years of memorable mornings in swamps, fields, boats, and the turkey woods—through a history of hunts combined now with this one, with my daughter.

It was a saga that had begun when I saw him and his son under that oak tree, as I drove up in his backyard. "Thanks, Herbie," I said. "Great job. Maybe the best I've ever seen you do, and that's saying something. Sarah, you nailed him!" I shouted again.

"Daddy, why did you run to him?"

"I didn't want him to get away, but I knew he wasn't going anywhere. I still wanted to make sure," I awkwardly tried to fabricate a reason a grown man would do such a thing.

Herb interrupted, "I was going to kill both of you if somebody didn't pull a trigger!" We all laughed. We posed for pictures with the gobbler spread out in front of us on the hedgerow, then I slung him over my shoulder, and we headed back to the cabin. I've had many memorable walks out of the woods: one with my first squirrel at twelve years old, several with setters and pointers and old hunting friends with vests full of bobwhites, one with the first turkey I called for myself on our farm, and a bunch with Herb after glorious duck hunts, some of them in blowing snow. But none has been as wondrous nor as rewarding as strolling there that late afternoon with a good friend and my daughter, listening to her reliving the whole thing as only a young girl can do, and listening to Herb jab her about almost throwing up. All three of us rejoiced in our own perceptions of the last hour, as only the moment itself could uniquely instill in each of us.

Sometime during the walk to the cabin, I looked over at Herb through Sarah's chattering and constant recounting that was going on between us, and we both laughed. We knew she was hooked on this eternal journey of a hunter. We had successfully passed it onto another, a good deed done in our waning years. Somehow, as if back in my own youth—even if just momentarily—the grass seemed greener, the clearing sky shouted a more vibrant blue, the sprouting buds busted forth stronger into the reviving spring woods and the glinting late afternoon sun illuminated all of us in a warmer glow.

Although Sarah repeatedly blasted the silence with an avalanche of excitedly blurted renditions of what had just transpired, the woods and field paused for a moment, saluting the scene of two old hunters walking with a new one, bringing her into the fold. Above the racket, there was reverence for a new birth. When we got to the cabin, Herb hoisted the great bird and hung him from the porch. Tradition required that he be displayed there for some period of time, just in case somebody drove up and dared ask the question, "Who shot him?" thus wading into the quicksand of another hour-long summary of what had just happened—from each of us. But nobody else came. We took more pictures, and then Herb fried rockfish cubes and prepared mashed potatoes for us, all with his special seasoning. Not usually a fish-eater, Sarah ate until she was stuffed.

During dinner, as mandated by traditional hunting laws, we all told, retold, and retold the same story. Sarah and I discussed the possibility of her going hunting again the following week but after thoughtful consideration, she stated, "I think it's better I don't go again for a while and give somebody else a chance."

My prideful glance over to Herb confirmed we agreed. "Okay, Sarah. I think that's fine," I acknowledged. After dinner, we all settled down in bed. Sarah went to sleep quickly and like usual, I did not come close to beating Herb to sleep. But as I lay there reading, I relived the entire afternoon; the gobblers slowly materializing from the hedgerow, then marching their determined wobbly-walk to us; Sarah breathing so hard that the gun was shaking; our whispering while trying to keep the birds from getting spooked; my little girl reaching down deep and making her mind up to finally shoot; and above all else, the hug she and I shared afterward and the broad infectious smile on her face as she told and retold her story. I said a little prayer of thanks for being able to experience such a great afternoon with my maturing daughter and a good friend. This was meant to be; too many things had to fall into place. I had to meet Herb; I had to buy Luke; with God's miracle blessing, Susan and I had to have Sarah; Sarah had to want to hunt; it went on and on. A full circle had to be completed and perseverance tested until the right time was indeed reached. And like so many other times in my hunting past, it all came together in a perfect moment. What had begun the day I drove up in Herb's yard and watched him there under the oak tree helping his own son shoot the turkey target, had now come full circle fifteen years later with me sitting under a pine tree, shoulder to shoulder with my daughter, while Herb helped coax in two gobblers. Yes, what goes around comes around, and history does repeat itself. Another memory added, I turned out the light and listened to the owls hooting in the low ground timber outside the cabin.

The next morning, Herb and I imitated them while scouting for more longbeards. Our season was about to open in less than a week.

Cabins

I have never stayed in any of the top ten hotels in the world, but I have spent a few nights at the Breakers in Palm Beach, cozied a quaint two evenings at a famous B&B in Aspen, and crashed more than one weekend at a Ritz Carlton. They're all very nice abodes, complete with scented and warmed towels, muffins on your pillows, bed turndowns, house robes for sale, and expensive gift shops. And yes, I did enjoy my stay in each of them and even ordered pizza and sat with my bride on the balcony of the B&B in Aspen after an all-day hike in the Maroon Bells. "We sure rednecked up this swank locale, didn't we?" I asked my new wife, as I reposed with a Dominos and boss Pepsi, while propping my feet up on the rail and taking in the Aston Martins cruising the main drag below us.

"Yes, we did. Do you want this last piece?" came her reply.

Do not get me wrong, I do appreciate the finer venues where one can simply forget about life's troubles—except for the bill of course—and let superior service and luxurious accommodations spoil one into thinking he or she could actually live like that all the time. It is indeed nice, for a while. But I will tell you that none of those establishments can hold a candle to some of the ramshackle hunting, fishing, and woodsy cabins I've stayed in over the last forty years. Maybe that rough pine A-frame on New Lake didn't have warm towels delivered, and maybe that shack on a hidden lake off Alligator River was about to fall into the water and perhaps that farmhouse fifteen miles east of Stuttgart had a snorer that made an Iron Maiden concert seem like Lawrence Welk popping bubbles on Saturday night at 7:00 p.m. back in the day, but all the memorable cabins where I've camped over the years had the intangibles. They were not just places to lay your head, they were sanctuaries fortified with heavy quilt blankets under which you constantly switched pillows while turning, squirming, and lying there in anticipation of the next morning—or reliving the gill snatches, retrieves, wing-cuppings or thundering gobbles of the previous day. I never went to bed in an expensive hotel so utterly excited that I could not sleep because I just might catch a record bass, or kill a mess of ducks, or shoot that nice eight-pointer the next morning. I slept like a log in those hotels. And I slept like

I was on a log at most of my cabins—not because the beds were uncomfortable but because I couldn't wait to get out of bed, get out of that cabin and into the world it represented.

Hunting and fishing and backwoods cabins are not just four walls and a roof, they're hallowed structures carefully enclosing, caressing, and preserving some of our best memories. Fancy hotels and B&Bs are five-course meals with white linen, a spoon carefully placed horizontally above your second plate and clear drinks with vermouth or Grey Goose. Cabins are bacon and eggs, pork chops, rock fish cubes, venison stew, oysters, rib eyes, and brown liquor or Mic Light, and Canada geese honking outside as they fly through a November sky silhouetted against a full moon. And I would just as soon warm my own towels by the fire pit, thank you.

One of the first times I ever stayed in a true woods cabin was as a guest of a hunting club near New Lake, in Hyde County. The small house was built right on the edge of the lake and the club was set up for a deer hunting and sometimes bear hunting, not necessarily my cup of tea at that time in my life since I was more into chasing partridges. But I was also all about getting off the beaten path and back in the woods any chance I could. So, every once in a while, my buddy let me tag along and quail hunt at the other end of the property while he was in a deer stand. After he climbed down from his stand and I put the dogs in the dogbox for the last time, we'd reconvene at the cabin that evening and grill streaks, or skin deer or dress quail—or all three. The cabin was four miles removed from any paved road, made from rough-hewn wood with a small deck built on the lake side and lined inside with several bunks made from two-by-sixes. It was rudimentarily constructed, but it had all the necessities needed for a weekend closer to the wilds. I never shot a deer at that club, nor do I recall bagging many quail, although my setter did point a few steaming purple berry-pies left by the ample bear population.

In the middle of an otherwise non-threatening bird hunt, few things will get your attention more than pushing through waist high purple berries and finding a steaming pile just feet in front of you. It gets you looking around and makes you a little edgy, especially in fading light. There are only so many animals that can leave such an unnerving invitation. Although there were those moments of heightened awareness, the main thing I remember about that cabin is lying in my bunk and listening to the almost deafening sound of giant waterfowl roosting on the lake. Swan, the beautiful, elegant white announcers of winter from the northern tundra, fly thousands of miles each year to arrive in our area of the country. All of us stop to look up when we hear them call. It's a good feeling. You know winter is here. You respect the voyage they have just endured, tip your hat to them, and welcome them for a few weeks; they're a returning annual guest, sort of like the cross-country cousin coming home for Christmas each year. But there are two things you don't do. You don't eat them if I cook them; nor would my dog eat the only one I ever shot. And you do not, or cannot, doze off in silence when you go to bed within 200 yards of them roosting on New Lake. They honk, cackle, groan, moan, and otherwise flare up all night. Don't get me wrong, it's beautiful, especially when there's a full moon over that still-secluded puzzling body of water that probably was formed when a peat-fueled fire burnt down into the coastal plain landscape thousands of years ago. Nobody knows for sure how it got there, or how its sister lakes like Phelps and Mattamuskeet, or the Carolina Bay lakes like White Lake, Jones and Singletary Lakes further south actually came to be.

Unlike some of the other lakes, there is no development clogging New Lake's shores. When you step out into a twenty-degree winter chill at 1:00 a.m., then gaze out onto the lake and see those giant necks outlined against the shimmering water with all kinds of raucousness going on, right there you know you are visiting a time witnessed first by Native Americans, and by few ever since. It is true nature; and you have found it right there amidst what was once a primordial undrained and unaltered pocosin. Lying at the headwaters of the Alligator, it is still pristine, and it still harkens to the fresh visitors from the far North—just like it did 1,000 years ago when the Native Americans paddled its shores in dugouts. Not much game was taken around that New Lake cabin by me, although I did help skin a few deer. But the feeling I got those December nights when the snowy white flocks rested out on the water, directed in their murmurs by the full moon, will always be in the recesses of my memory; the far back places reserved for undiluted instincts and primeval responses to nature's last provocations in this too-worldly world.

Cabins have a way of doing that. They occupy woods, fields, lakes, and mountains that you remember, and they linger in the back forty of your mind like a ghostly buck skirting the edge of a pre-rut swamp. It's not the floor joists, nor the roof, nor the walls that you think about when you reminisce about that favorite cabin; it's the surroundings. What did you do there? What ordeal did you endure, or what joy did you experience? If the construction of the cabins was important, you wouldn't look back fondly upon them. Shoot, you probably would have never stayed in them in the first place. Some of the shacks were not fit for a dog. But it didn't matter because you were there to rough it, to get back to that genuine person obscured by the facade your soul hides behind when you walk in the city and follow the human beat too long.

One such cabin—or really half-cabin half-houseboat, and all-dilapidated shack—was on a hidden lake just off Alligator River. Although I'd worked around Alligator River one summer when I was in college, taking peat samples for our geology department, I'd never fished the Alligator. So, when some buds asked me to go with them on an overnight fishing trip in the spring of '96 and reminded me we would be hitting the raccoon perch spawning season right on the nose, and that we would fry them up on the bank, spend the night in a shack on a hidden lake and tell each other lies, I spurted, "Sign me up!"

Putting in at Gum Neck: three boats, six guys and enough gear to go up the Amazon in 1905, we made our way across the upper reaches of the Alligator, across the Inland Waterway and over to what was supposedly the general area of the entrance to the lake. We stopped in the middle of river and regrouped. "It's right over there," came the assured directives of one of those in the party who had hunted and fished there before.

Neither I nor my boat mate had ever been to the lake, and we could not make out the entrance that our Roosevelt-like leader was supposedly distinguishing from the rest of the Cretaceous-looking bank. Nonetheless, following the other two boats, we carefully picked our way through the numerous cypress stumps lining the shore. Sure enough, there in front of us and curving back to the south, was a small canal entrance. All three boats started in.

Cruising up the winding canal where palmettos lined the bank like some impenetrable army guarding its territory, our flotilla must have resembled something out of a Johnny Quest opening scene. The only thing lacking was head-hunters in canoes chasing us and jaguars leaping onto us from overhanging limbs. Instead, there were squirrels jumping limb to limb overhead and waves launched from our cutting bows splashing against the jungle bank and spraying us on their return trip against our hull. It felt like we were on an expedition looking for Mayan riches. We zigged and zagged our way for a mile or so. Suddenly, the narrow sinuous channel opened up into a lost brackish lake. While strategies were mapped over idling engines, I couldn't help but gaze at the cypress, junipers, and gum trees growing around and falling into the edges of the water. *What peacock bass look-a-likes there must be here*, I thought. We all agreed to go to the cabin, unload and then fish.

• • •

The shack itself was precariously balanced on pilings that had been slammed into the peaty bottom by a timber company eons ago.

It was a one-room, rat-infested off-square leaner with noticeable rot and decay. But the roof was intact and the dock, also serving duty as the front porch, was a good place to sit and drink a beer. *It was perfect.* We all threw our sleeping bags inside, rigged the poles and headed out to different coves off the main body. The perch started hitting immediately. Rarely did we cast and not catch one. Occasionally, a jack or dark bass would hit. We finished the first day with upwards of fifty perch.

Later that night, with jackets turned up around our necks against the remaining March chill, we fried fish and listened to the owls while everyone told at least one lie—with a few of the zealots telling more than their fair share. It was black that night; black swamp air, black water, and the coal black timber swallowed us whole. We had a couple of lanterns and a fire, but we were surrounded by total darkness broken only by the brilliant stars. But the conversation, knee slaps, winks and possum grins lit everything up, and made the scurrying mice not such a big deal after we turned in.

She creaked under our weight, and I guess if you thought about it, there was a chance, if not probability, she would collapse right into the lake with all six of us in there. But we didn't think of that. Instead, we squirmed, enduring the wait for the next morning's first cast.

There is something about stars and cabins. Maybe it's because the best cabins are often in remote areas, where you can actually see the stars vs. some mall parking lot where you can only see the fluorescent reminders of our own superficiality. Or maybe it's because most of my memories are during the cooler months when you can more clearly see how small we really are as you look up to that clear cold sky. Whatever the reason, stars are always there, peering down at cabins, winking their approval, and signaling to you that they have briefly allowed you into this world that so few dare to enter.

Thousands of light years away, they are perhaps the best mirror we have for ourselves. Since Sarah was a little girl, during the fall and winter months, we have periodically taken her to the back of the farm fields at night, cut off the truck and the lights and got out. "Look up," we say. "What do you see?"

Answers over the years have changed from "stars" to just silence.

Exactly.

The most brilliant and impressive night sky I ever saw east of the Rockies was very early one January morning in 1995. I was working on the Outer Banks and a customer had invited me to go duck hunting with him out on the Sound. He and his buddies, all locals from the island, which meant Hatteras Island in those parts back then, owned grandfathered hunting rights to some remaining curtain blinds built into the shoals.

That morning, I left Kill Devil Hills at 3:00 a.m. and drove south across Oregon Inlet, through Rodanthe, and toward Buxton. In winter, there are no lights in the straight stretches between the lower Dare County towns and that night the stars were shining like a million sparklers. I could see the actual curvature of the earth, as I looked west from the Sound toward the ocean in the east. I drove forty miles per hour, just taking in the vista and hoping to see as many shooting stars as possible. Sure enough, ten blistered the sky that night, more than I'd ever seen in one night. Without any warning, these momentary lessons in astrophysics tutored only to hunters, fishermen, campers, and explorers who routinely and passionately venture away from so-called "civilization" represented by electronic dingings, lighted city streets, and neurotic celebrities, shot briefly north and northeast. You could see from Bermuda to Asheville that night; it was sort of like looking at a picture taken with one of those fisheye lenses that render a curved panorama. Everyone needs to take a ride like that each year. It puts you and everything around you in perspective. We may think we are the cat's meow with our fancy skyscrapers, electric cars, international financial agreements and skinny suits, but when you gaze up into the black winter sky stretching from mainland to the ocean you find a new perspective. There's nothing like driving south down Highway 12 in the middle of a clear cold night in January, every second eagerly anticipating another lavender shooting star careening tangentially off the outer reaches of the atmosphere. That's when you absolutely know where you stand in this world. Try it. The TV and your cell phone will not seem so important.

The boat ride to the shoals was choppy and salty spray continually pelted us over the center console windshield. Although I grew up just across the Sound from where we were bouncing, I stood there gripping the console like a pilgrim from Kansas alongside those guys from Frisco, Buxton, and Hatteras. As the grayness approached, we arrived at a plank cabin set on pilings a good mile from shore. It was fifteen feet above the water and equipped with table and chairs, a propane cook-stove, heater, and windows. We docked the boat and scampered up the stairs with our gear and quickly decided who should go to the blind first. I sat there with my host and watched as the dawn emerged from behind us and 500 yards away, the first rafts piled over the curtain blind and on top of the first hunters. Wave after wave of pintails, redheads, widgeon, and blackheads hovered over that blind. My host and I watched from the comfort of the cabin as the ducks, seeing for the first time the hunters rise up, seemingly from the water itself, backed up like horses rearing in a corral. Pretty soon, it was our turn.

We made the short skiff ride to the blind. It's a weird feeling getting out onto a shoal in the middle of the Sound, one mile from shore, with Hatteras inlet visibly breaking waves to the south. And when you step down below the water's surface and into an adjustable blind built from salt-treated one-by-sixes and rubber membranes rendering you chest level with the surface of the water, it's actually a little unnerving—until the first rafts come barreling in, a mere two feet off the water. I've had many duck hunts in my day, but that hunt in a curtain blind with my head only inches above the water and ducks not knowing you were there until the absolute last minute, was one of the highlights of my long hunting career. I still have a pintail on the wall in our old store as evidence of that morning in a famed Pamlico Sound curtain blind. But more prominent than that duck over my chair is the memory of that entire hunt; the cabin on stilts, the bacon cooking, the cold biting January Pamlico Sound wind, the shooting stars on a lonely Outer Banks drive, and the novelty of it all. I have only been to that cabin out on the shoals once, but its location is one I always find on a map when the cold fronts of November start swirling.

During Thanksgiving of 2001, I was reminded just how far those winds of the Sound can travel. I flew to Stuttgart, Arkansas to duck hunt with a good friend that year. Neither of us had ever been there and when another friend said he wanted to book a guided two-day hunt for all of us in the rice field impoundments east of Stuttgart, we trusted his decision and went for it.

Driving fifteen miles outside of Stuttgart, we turned up a gravel road and drove another five miles to an old farmhouse that had been renovated into a hunting lodge. There were three rooms holding up to four hunters each. The accommodations were not luxurious but certainly adequate. After unpacking that first night in camp, we all sat around talking, discussing the next day and waiting on the arrival of the last group.

They walked in about 8:00 p.m. and after putting up their gear, settled down with us in the living room. We all introduced ourselves and began the usual, "Where are y'all from?" conversation. The new group said they were from Wilmington, North Carolina.

"Really?" we replied. "We're all from North Carolina, too."

As the conversation progressed and having hunted Stump Sound and a gamelands just north of Wilmington, I asked the late arrivals where they hunted.

"Actually, we hunt north of Wilmington, about halfway up the coast," came the reply.

"Seriously? Where?" I asked, knowing that their answer might just put them in the vicinity of some of my hunting spots.

"Oh, a little town you've probably never heard of."

"Give me a shot," I countered.

"You ever heard of Mesic?"

I about spit out my grown-up beverage across the White River into Memphis. "Oh yeah, I know where Mesic is," I replied. "I grew up in Maribel just west of there. Where do you hunt in Mesic?"

To make a long story short, they hunted in the same creek where I grew up hunting and had even met one of the locals and, subsequently, had entered into a "discussion" with him." I knew the whole story . . . and it weren't pretty. That's still my absolute best "small world" story ever. The duck hunting was good—not flooded timber, but good. The food was wholesome, not Dominos in Aspen but adequate. Except for the world record snorer in the bunk next to me who was trying to call in rutting moose, it was a good experience.

"But what are the odds," I asked my friend that night, of us coming halfway across the country, driving fifteen miles from the nearest city and then driving five miles up a dirt road, only to run into a guy that hunts the creek where I used to hunt?"

"Probably the same as Iron Maiden there hushing up," was the reply, as we both stared at the farmhouse ceiling, wishing we'd brought more pillows to stuff against our bombarded ears.

No matter how far back you're off a farm road in the middle of the flatlands of eastern Arkansas, or how close you are to a highway in eastern North Carolina for that matter, it's a small world among hunters, and an even smaller world in a snored-up cabin.

• • •

One of my favorite hunting cabins is five miles off the highway and nestled amongst a group of other hunting shacks. A few of them are over a hundred years old and rough-cut out of virgin cypress logs. This assemblage of small houses surrounds a members' clubhouse and is located on the floodplain of the Roanoke, one of eastern North Carolina's most venerable rivers. Surrounding all the cabins is a 3,000-acre utopia for big deer and old gobblers. When the water is right and the weather bears down from the north, it can be some of the best duck hunting in the state.

I was introduced to this family cabin by a good friend. At that time, it was owned by him and two friends of his recently deceased father. They all took me in, and I got to relive all the old hunting stories through the tales of two fine older gentlemen. I didn't spend much time with them, but John and Aubrey were from the old school. With my friend's father, they had seen the cabin through the glory years of the 1960s and 1970s and would eventually pass it on to my friend, his family and acquaintances.

I spent many nights in that cabin, relishing in dinners of baked rockfish, homemade cabbage slaw, hand-rubbed backstrap, double baked potatoes, and adult beverages—all bolstered by myriad stories conjuring up all the old haunts of the club. I came to know most of the locales myself. I busted an old gobbler with beard rot there at Turkey Pond and missed one at Duck Pond in a slough where an older gentleman had once built an elevated duck blind way up in a tree back in the 1940s. I'd sat on a few deer stands around the Canal Road and hunted mallards in the Cut Down. I'd joined in the large clubhouse dinners with all the members, whiffing the fireplace smoke wafting from cut-up oak blowdowns, and I'd helped clean paths during workdays. I'd even helped renovate the old cabin when my friend finally owned it outright.

As we cleaned out the attic of that cabin, I told him that I'd never in my life seen so many dirt-dauber nests. "Some of these got dirt from Krakatoa in 'em. We'll certainly freeze to death without this insulation!" I kidded him.

The floor creaked, tar seeped through the porch boards, and the old oil heater pinged as she came to life during the cold nights. But for a few years during the height of my ducking days, the experiences there were unmatched. One particular night, my buddy and I both drove straight from our work locations to the cabin and arrived after dark in a 53-degree December drizzle. "The weatherman is calling for snow tomorrow morning, Bill," I was informed, as I threw my bag on the bed and undid my tie.

"Well, he's an idiot," I proclaimed. "It's 53 degrees, bud."

After an ample dinner of baked lasagna, we hit the sack—not even contemplating there may be white stuff falling the next day.

As we rolled out of bed a few hours later, my friend looked at the thermometer on the back porch and said, "Ah Bill, it's 28 degrees outside."

"You're kidding me!" I replied, peeking out the front door. To my astonishment, I saw what I did not expect. Swallowing an unusually delightful bit of crow meat, I slammed back. "Guess what, bud. It's snowing! Let's roll, and quick!"

We shoved coffee down our throats, grabbed the gear, canoe, and dogs and headed to the flooded Cut Down. The quacking of new arrivals with snow on their tails was roaring, as we arrived. That hunt is another story, but let's just say it was one for the books. Whenever I see that cabin, I think about the nights spent snuggled under covers, waiting for the cacklings of the dawn. I think about my dog Luke waiting outside in his cozy dogbox, knowing in his own dog ways what the morning could be. I think about the delicious meals we ate, the owls hooting in the low ground and the excitement the bottomland always gave us the next morning. I think about sitting in the 1950 art deco metal chair on the front porch with my bud and my daughter—she kidding him about the number of inappropriate words he'd used during the previous two minutes. She subsequently won our bet, giggling when she told my bud I was paying her per word.

That red one-story house with the addition in the back and the covered front porch is small. But it holds big memories that are always at the forefront of my thoughts—and not just for me.

Not all cabins represent spectacular hunts, unending fish stringers or family gatherings. Some are frankly very forgettable, but they remain engraved on our minds, intruders into an otherwise august world of warm nostalgia. They are lowly mergansers, or "hoods" as we call them, zipping into a cupped-up flock of late-season greenies.

One night in November of 1996, I drove to one of my absolute favorite places, historic Lake Mattamuskeet, to hunt ducks with a recent acquaintance, and some other dudes whom I didn't know. It poured a cold soaking rain the whole way down. If you've never driven from Columbia to Fairfield in a driving rain that's been deluging for a couple of days, let me tell you, that road can get pretty soggy on all sides. There are no lights on that two-lane rock road and, after the sun goes down, it's as black as a pocosin bear on a moonless night. It looked like the whole twenty-mile road was just one spindly bridge over one massive impoundment. I was convinced we could have set decoys right off the road and shot ducks the next day. I was equally concerned that if we ran off the road, they wouldn't find us until the next fall when everything dried out—after the beans were picked. We arrived at the flashing light in Fairfield that night as probably the first people ever to consider that quaint community to be high ground. Then we had the unenviable task of finding the cabin. Our directions were, "It's somewhere in the woods beside the lake." Yep, that's about all we had. Oh yeah, and my passenger had stayed there—once. We finally found it.

It was an added-on, half-falling-down, half-rotten shack packed with too many hunters. We walked in and I immediately grasped that as the newbie, I would be sleeping on the kitchen floor. Yep, that spongy pile of peeling linoleum with the dirt all over it, except what I thought at first glance was excessive loose dirt, turned out to be enough mouse droppings to make the Carlsbad Caverns bats jealous. Sure enough, those little devils ran across my North Face bag all night. I didn't sleep, thinking about those teal we might shoot the next day.

The next morning, we did shoot a few teal. We even hunted on the Lake proper after walking 300 yards through muck so thick and sticky that I thought I was going to need two knee replacements at what I now consider to be the boyish age of thirty-six.

We left Mattamuskeet later in the afternoon in penultimate seventy-five-degree weather, with only a few ducks to show for our venture. It was an adequate finale to a balmy duck-lacking day with the memory of the absolute most miserable cabin within which I ever camped palling over me. But it's a story, and we were ducking at one of the most beautiful water fowling spots of all time—so all else is secondary.

Contrary to the infamous Mattamuskeet shack, which squats barely three feet above sea level during low tide at Engelhard, my favorite cabin perches on a hill surrounded by a 1,000-acre ranch in northwest Colorado. When I visited that cabin, the owners—friends of my wife's parents, who'd recently celebrated their sixty-seventh wedding anniversary—called it the "Hill House," so that is what my wife and I call it. It's an A-framed 800-square-foot structure that would be identified as a chalet in the Alps or Crested Butte, if it had AC, heat, or electricity. It has none of those. But it does have a balcony off the second floor where my new bride and I sat one night, serenaded by the wildness of coyotes howling and barking their acknowledgment of the vibrant stars settled so low above the peaks that it looked like you could reach out and touch them. If there had been a northeast wind that night, you could have heard them all the way to Grand Junction. But it was so still that even when we readjusted our position in our chairs, we did it very carefully and deliberately, trying not to echo our intruding presence and thus disturbing the altar prepared for us. We sat, sometimes in silence, scanning in awe from the farthest star to the nearest sage. We did not move much. We talked very low, almost whispering, but still communicated with each other that night as well as we ever have—sometimes without saying a word. We were respectful of where we were, of both the natural beauty that captivated us and of the exciting time in our lives. Other than the stars, the only light for miles was the lantern reflecting through the window of the lower cabin where our hosts stayed, their experienced beacon of reassurance shining through a dark night and upon our upcoming road of marriage. There was a stalwart September mountain coolness calming over the pines and aspens that night, and over that balcony, as well.

Just off to the side of the Hill House, there's a path that leads to a mountain, or another "hill," as the locals call it in western Colorado. Of course, they weren't raised in the lowlands of eastern North Carolina where a "mountain" is anything taller than the Federal Courthouse in New Bern and a "hill" is full of fire ants. At the top of this mountain behind the Hill House, there's a perfect spot nestled into the brush where two honeymooners sat at dawn the next morning and watched majestic bull elk valiantly court nearly willing cows across a 400-yard meadow, bugling to each other and challenging the very bane of each other's existence. The yellow aspens were peaking, and the fresh fall Colorado air was filling our straining lungs. Like a thin veil, a faint mist hung over the natural amphitheater below us, giving way to the rising sun as it drifted up the mountainsides, reluctantly revealing to us the pursued cows and one of the defiant bulls. The whole valley, or "bowl," as the owner called it, resounded in the high-pitched, nasally bull pleadings. Each bull would start his bellowing before another had finished, like a bunch of eager teenage boys pushing each other aside to flex their muscles in front of a covey of blushing young girls. There were so many bulls hammering that from our vantage point a quarter mile away, we could never pinpoint which one was actually bugling, nor narrow down his exact location in the dark timber. Those bugles still reverberate in my ears, and when I see an elk stretching his neck and drawing up his sides on one of the hunting shows, I always stop what I'm doing and listen. It is one of nature's true beckoning's, irresistibly summoning us to partake in its Rocky Mountain grandeur—a harkening that is matched only by the bobwhite call. The non-stop activity lasted an hour and a half until the whole herd decided to bluster through the aspens to another ranch. Feeling blessed to have witnessed such a spectacular event, we also knew we were fortunate just to have been there and to have made the plane flight out.

We'd started our honeymoon on September 19, 2001, and the tenseness that existed at the airport was palpable when we departed Raleigh. Everyone wore American flag pins or displayed a patriotic sticker on their belongings. Susan and I had a chance to cancel the entire trip the day after 9/11. All the hotels and accommodations we had booked were understanding and gave us ample chance to back out. But we decided to make our own little stand a week after the tragic events in New York, D.C., and Shanksville. And we went. That Hill House cabin and the ranch it overlooks will always be in the back of my mind. The coyotes at night, the stars, the majestic elk, the meadow in that hidden bowl, the Rockies at dawn and the mist rising through the peaking yellow aspens screaming their season's last breaths, all stay with me daily. Not just a joyous experience in nature, the Hill House represents to me a moment in time when I knew I had made right decisions, decisions to be with my new bride on that balcony—to be with her anywhere, and the decision we had indeed made to go on our honeymoon. We had "gone for it" and it had worked.

A year later when we were trying to have Sarah through in-vitro, I would reach back for that feeling I had on that balcony in Colorado. And once again, God would grace us with his presence. Yes, that cabin is special. And it's not on a hill, it's on the tallest mountain I know—one that reaches as close to God as I have ever been.

• • •

Cabins are not structures. They're emotions wrapped in old worn lumber, histories protected by rusty tin and big hearty greetings covered by overhanging porches. Cabins are the pinging of cast iron woodstoves and the popping of fireplaces melting into bellowing laughter, following told and retold stories; they are squeaky floors meshing with the clanging of dishes being washed after a feast; they're the smell of old coats and vests and orange and camo hats mixed with peppered fried chicken and twice-baked potatoes from the oven. Cabins are the reflections of red coals of a December fire dancing upon the smooth wind-burned faces of children being raised right, and against the weathered faces of those raising them. Cabins are integral to this life we all love as outdoorsmen. They envelope our memories as guardians of our past, and as protectors of the history we pass on. And if you look close enough, amongst the old photos, the spent shotgun shells placed on shelves, the animal mounts on the walls, the old Herter's compass hanging on a nail, the dog collars of past faithful, the South Bend reel here or the Shur-Shot box there, they are breathing monuments to the very life that sustains us. Never turn down the chance to stay in a cabin. You may never know what lies just beyond its doors.

Uncle Simmons

Nobody visits anymore. Those of us who were "raised right," as we say in these parts, struggle when this reality pops into our mind. Because we saw our parents make the effort to spend quality time with neighbors and relatives, including children, we wonder why we cannot do the same. Unlike us, our parents were probably not hemmed in by the start of some precious football game or sidetracked by a must-have weekly trip to the mall. Similarly, it's doubtful they even cared about such captivating issues as who might win the next Dancing with the Bachelorette and it's a safe bet they weren't terrified by the unthinkable social consequences of taking time away from pretentious mingling at the Club. We've all made excuses why we don't make the effort anymore. Too often, we're mere commentators on our own internal battles of conscientious versus laziness, passively enabling laziness to win in sloppily played games, and always knowing there will be another contest next week. Is it really too bothersome to stop our rat race just long enough to relate to people, like was done back-in-the-day? When I was a child, you knew your neighbors, and you helped them. Adults assisted each other and they all made sure kids were brought along slow and straight. Like a burgeoning oak on a swamp ridge, we children were given proper light and nurtured in hopes that one day we would be tall and strong. We were not just plucked down in rows and expected to make a quick return, like a loblolly on a pine plantation. We were a long-term investment in the future of all of us, and we were treated as such. I'm not saying we should put anyone, especially children, on a pedestal and kowtow to their every perceived need. Nor do I propose we should be our children's "friends," placing them at the center of conversation and getting to know all of their idols like is done by cool parents these days. Goodness, I can honestly say that neither my mother nor my stepfather ever asked me about the latest gossip on Linda Ronstadt. Actually, I didn't care about that stuff, myself, as long as I could look at her and listen to her. Her flirtations with whomever she was courting didn't matter to me as long as I could keep her poster on my wall and play her *Prisoner in Disguise* eight-track in my Vega—and, of course, fish or squirrel hunt. I'm not a psychologist, but I do think much of the so-called expert psycho-hyperbole floating around today actually weakens children, giving them a false sense of their overall importance in this world. Don't get me wrong, my teenage daughter is indeed the apple of the universe to me and my wife, but I'm not going to read up on whatever teen knucklehead she is currently following on Facechat, just so I can be "chill." But she is still going to be in the woods with her daddy; she will keep learning to shoot and we will always have our one-on-one conversations about what really matters. And hopefully, she'll have a genuine boost toward being a strong young woman because of it.

I'm not sure any of us actually realizes how important these special interactions can be. Many times, we just go about our daily hustle-bustle lives, heading over a cliff of oblivion toward a lemming wasteland of insignificant busyness. It really just takes a few minutes of quality time spent with the right person, in the right environment, at the right time in their lives—and it can make a lifetime of difference.

• • •

Uncle Simmons was the third boy born to Clyde and Mary Elizabeth "Miss Mini" Fentress. My first memory of him was being lifted up onto his broad shoulders, exalted by my new-found hierarchy over the small world around me, but also a little intimidated by his strong hands and booming, well-defined voice. He stood six feet tall with short blondish hair and a distinctive nose, but it was his voice that I remember most.

"Adolf, what do you think of this four-year-old growing boy?" he would ask my Granddaddy, holding me high. He always called Granddaddy "Adolf"—not "Daddy," not "Father," not "Pop,"—just "Adolf."

I asked Mom one day why he did not call Granddaddy, "Daddy." I was old enough by then to know that Hitler had been a terrible dictator, so Mom confided to me that it was Uncle Simmons' way of kidding Granddaddy because in Uncle Simmons's judgment, my sure-minded grandfather had a tendency to order everybody around. I understood what she meant. Although he'd been wounded in WWI and had sent one son from the farm to fight Hitler in WWII, my normally stoic granddaddy actually did enjoy the banter. Standing there with Uncle Simmons's arm around his shoulder and being referred to as a supreme dictator, Granddaddy would every once in a while—just occasionally—break a rare smile. Still, the idea of jabbing with your parent was foreign to me when I was a child.

Of course, when I was in my early twenties and Mom was working feverishly on her genealogy research, I warned her regularly that one day, amid all of her deed searches, marriage license inquiries, and cemetery visits, she would find some long-lost cousin whose ancestry she wished we were not connected to. Sure enough, she found a horse thief in our family. It's in the genes, I suppose—the jabbing, not the horse thievery. Uncle Simmons was always kidding and joking and laughing; he'd cut a sly grin here and sneak a flashy glance there, winking to make sure you caught his quickness and reveling when you did. This mischievous sense of humor and sharp wit probably helped him immensely in his career as a news correspondent.

After attending Wake Forest, and becoming a Neiman Fellow at Harvard, he first worked with the *News and Observer* in Raleigh, then *The Charlotte Observer*, and later became Atlanta Bureau Chief for *Time Magazine* in the 1960s. Among other prevalent stories during those turbulent times, he also covered the racial strife in the deep South. While I don't know all the details, I remember Mom telling me, "That was when the first Fentress was promptly thrown into jail." Mom had her own wit too. I never got the complete story, but my understanding was that Uncle Simmons may have asked the wrong question of the wrong person at the wrong time.

Though he was raised in the South, a proper upbringing, years of education and refinement of interviewing skills had not only set in him deep beliefs regarding the status of race relations, it had weaned him away from some of the typical country colloquialisms. He had sort of a noncommittal Maryland accent and my guess is that his mid-Atlantic dialect did not necessarily help him nestle up to the pot-bellied stoves at every country store. After Atlanta, and at a time when the Vietnam War was escalating in 1967, Uncle Simmons became Saigon Bureau Chief for *Time*. The decision to take that promotion was not an easy one for him. Not only was it potentially dangerous, he would be far from home for two years, was not be able to visit his aging parents nor hunt and fish, and most importantly, was separated from Aunt Ruth for long periods. Even though Aunt Ruth stayed in Hong Kong during that time,

Uncle Simmons was mostly in Saigon reporting on the growing conflict. They were apart a lot; Aunt Ruth sent us letters, pictures, and occasional gifts, and we would get an infrequent note from Uncle Simmons, but we did not see him for two years.

When he finally assumed new duties for *Time* in Washington, D.C., and returned to the states permanently, we all gathered in my grandparents' living room one night to see his home movies of Saigon, his trip over to the street markets in Thailand and his visit to India and the Taj Mahal, complete with king cobras being charmed by the locals. Looming behind the pulsating eight-millimeter reel-to-reel like Cecil B. DeMille, Uncle Simmons commandingly narrated the goings-on like only he could do. "Now Adolf, those kids over there could give you a run for your money on salesmanship. You could really use them in the old store," he chided, winking at Mom.

"Billy, those boys charming those snakes are your age. What do you think about that?"

I was fascinated. I didn't understand exactly where the Taj Mahal was or how people bought live chickens and pigs right on the street, but it was an enlightening experience for a boy growing up in Maribel, North Carolina, who had only traveled as far as Raleigh to see the circus. I certainly had no grasp of Vietnam, nor was I aware of the political divisiveness and disruption that was transpiring in our country at that time. But after hearing Uncle Simmons describe how he'd been pushed into a fox hole by a protective sergeant during a Viet Cong attack, I sensed that there may be real danger out there beyond our sheltered life on the farm. And I realized he could have been hurt. Above all else, I was just glad he was back, and we could see more of him—like before his foray overseas.

Before Vietnam, when I was between the ages of five and seven, Uncle Simmons and Aunt Ruth would come home relatively often to see Granddaddy and Grandmamma and, of course, my sister, Betty, and me. For two children who had lost their father, Uncle Simmons's brother, the visit by somebody close to us, who paid unequivocal attention to us and who knew our father so well, was an event. Living way out in rural eastern North Carolina, we didn't have many visitors and our life revolved mostly around our country store and farm in our own little section of our county.

Our paternal grandmother and grandfather lived at the end of a small rocky lane behind us in a two-story early twentieth-century farmhouse built by my great-grandfather. My three great-aunts lived up the road about four miles where Betty and I regularly attended church under their tutoring, and my cousins lived in "Little Washington," as we called it, just an hour away. On my mom's side, many cousins were spread all over eastern North Carolina, and another grandfather and grandmother lived on a farm six miles to the west in Alliance. A tremendous support mechanism was well in place, and we never lacked for affection. We loved living where we lived and how we lived, despite the hardship of losing our father. Still, because Uncle Simmons took the time to be with us, and to be specifically with us, we got very excited whenever he came back home to visit.

One of those visits occurred in the spring of 1966. Excitedly anticipating his arrival that warm afternoon, my sister and I paced back and forth in the store, taking turns running outside to anxiously peer down the tree-lined lane toward Grandmamma's house. Scouting that little road like a couple of jackals waiting on a hare, we finally spotted Uncle Simmons as his car came to a stop under the pecan tree beside the azaleas in Grandmamma's yard. Mom almost had to chain us to the store counters to keep us from immediately sprinting down the road, arms flailing and mouths screaming, bombarding Uncle Simmons before he could even get the luggage out of the car. We knew we'd soon be enjoying something with him. Would it be fishing, or riding around the field roads, or would we go down to the river, or maybe he would get the guns out and shoot for us?

For him, it was surely a much-deserved escape from the city and a chance to get back to his roots, to the goodness of his boyhood earth—away from the pressures of deadlines and editors. For us, it was a chance to reconnect with someone who knew us and who was always overjoyed to see us. Finally, after Mom decided Uncle Simmons had at least been able to hug our grandmother, she let us go. Sun dappling our faces and mouths wide open, we hurtled down the little rock road in full anticipatory glee. Running up to him, we unleashed all of our pent-up exclamations, questions, and utter childishness.

He broke into his typical large grin. After the initial onslaught, hugs, and hellos, he first joked with Betty that the Beatles still didn't hold a candle to Sinatra, and then inquired about my latest strategies for arranging plastic toy Army men in the dirt beside the store. Uncle Simmons didn't have children, but he instinctively knew what we craved, and I think he understood better than we, our connection to the farm and to our dad. It really didn't matter what we did, it was always fun. After bags were put away and Aunt Ruth was settled, Uncle Simmons piled us into his car and drove us down to Swan Point, a favorite fishing spot. It's a true wonder how any fish at all remained in the river that day, given the decibels reached as we grabbed all the gear out of the boot and hustled down to the marsh. Buckets banging, rods clanging and tackle boxes scraping, we mucked through the greening marsh, laughing, catching up and eagerly anticipating the fresh breezes of the river ahead.

Once at the water's edge, we baited up, cast the rigs, set the rods in the holders, and then set out on one of our excursions. Uncle Simmons was never one to watch an inactive line too long; there were too many nesting redwing blackbirds to hear, too many longleaf cones to gather, too many shells to skip, too many pools to wade; there were too many boyhood memories on that shore for him to relive. He always wanted to explore and show us things. I'm sure he did a lot of walking in Atlanta and Washington, D.C., pounding the pavement between government office buildings and *Time* magazine, but I think when he got back to his roots, he just wanted to roam the fields and the riverbanks and take it all in. Perhaps he wanted to relive the innocence of different times, when men didn't die in wars or from cancer, and life in the country revolved around the changing tides and new seasons on the farm. Perhaps he wanted us to know the histories permeating those surroundings; the histories of three brothers. As usual, we methodically made our way around the shore, periodically pausing to peer down into the clear tannic water and scan the horizon toward the working trawlers. Uncle Simmons immersed both of us in stories about catching croakers, trout, and big drum right next to the bank and filled me with Jonah—dreams of outmuscling one of those bronze giants with my little black Zebco 202. Thinking I might spot a 75-pounder scowling up at me with a big fisheye, I sometimes lagged behind, as he and Betty marched on. But I didn't dare linger too long because I might miss something.

"Look at that seagull dive. Those redwings are really raising Cain over there in the marsh. I bet there are oysters off that point. Your daddy and I fished right over there when we were just a little older than you, Billy!" he rapidly interjected, as we plodded along the marsh.

Probably unknown to him, his audience was far more captivated than any readership could ever be. Betty and I were dedicated subscribers and though our subscription arrived only a few times a year, the quality of the experience was unmatched.

We explored the riverbank most of that afternoon, bathing in the pre-summer sun, scraping egg-white barnacles off graying driftwood, inspecting bubbling marsh-crab holes, dangling our feet in the cool water, and listening to the raucous gulls as they flew back and forth between tractors plowing in the coastal fields and the channel markers in the river. It was near perfect, and it was the way families should be. After we'd soaked in as much as we could, we packed up and headed back to the car. On the way out, I was talking about some long-ago forgotten topic that was important and interesting to me and supposedly to Uncle Simmons, but that I'm sure was a typical annoyance to my sister, when suddenly Uncle Simmons stopped.

"Listen," he shushed.

Betty was the first to hear it. "It's a bobwhite!" she whispered, excitedly.

Uncle Simmons glanced over with an approving professorial smile. "Let's see if we can hear all three notes," he suggested.

Sure enough, the quail started the first "bob" note very low, almost undetectably, and ended with the familiar "bobwhiieeete" two-note call.

"Isn't that just pretty?" Uncle Simmons exclaimed, hands on hips and looking up through the swaying trees, breathing it all in through his ample nose and pausing to listen for another call. And there was another, and another. That was the first time I'd heard a bobwhite and it was as if that hidden feathered gentleman was whistling directly to me, adding a little mystery to a tranquil afternoon.

Puckering and spewing, and encouraged by Uncle Simmons's attentive instruction, Betty and I practiced the three-note call all the way back to the car. We continued working on it the rest of the day.

From then on, I've always listened for the little partridges while walking the fields, and now when I do hear one, I stop and crane an ear for that barely audible first note—just like Uncle Simmons taught us. Birds weren't simply a pastime in our family, they were an integral part of our father's life. Chasing pointers was our dad's passion and although Uncle Simmons worked in the city, he always looked forward to coming home to walk the hedgerows with Daddy. It was a little connection he could pass on, and he did.

That same year, just before Christmas, Uncle Simmons returned to Maribel for another visit. Sauntering into the store wearing his canvas hunting coat, briar-proof pants and red wool cap, he had no trouble convincing my sister and me to cavort around the bean fields with him.

It was a cool bright December afternoon and given the growing excitement of the approaching present-filled morning combined with Uncle Simmons's visit, Betty and I were at a fever pitch. We had no bird dogs at that time, so we just followed behind Uncle Simmons, his devoted entourage excitedly plugging along behind its leader, like chicks following in line behind a mother quail. Bean stubble crunching under his long strides, he reminisced to us about where the old coveys used to be and how stubborn, tight-holding birds once flushed meteorically over our father's dog, Beau. Though my fellow hunters today would say the 1960s were in fact the good ol' days of quail hunting, he proclaimed then, as I do today, that, "There just aren't the birds there used to be."

Stooping down to our level, he also occasionally pointed out deer tracks and coon tracks whenever we came across them, making sure we knew how to tell a buck from a doe and a coon from a possum. But mostly that day, I remember our talking and laughing. Uncle Simmons was also asking us questions about our lives that we were all too happy to answer. Of course, he spent a career doing that. It was his job, and he was good at it. He was undeniably using the same refined journalistic probing techniques on Betty and me. But he knew it worked and it was genuine time spent with us, getting to know us better and probably vanquishing an inner need he had to ensure his brother's children could realize as much happiness as possible during his brief time with us. At the back of the field, I suddenly heard a large commotion in the brush and all kinds of pandemonium broke loose, as a large covey flushed and glided into the twisted honeysuckle at the head of Chapel Creek. Over a quarter century later, I would shoot the offspring of that same covey when I was in my thirties, hunting over my own setter. Uncle Simmons quickly shouldered his Remington and fired off a couple of shots. Frankly, I didn't understand what had just happened. I heard the rumble and saw Betty jump about six feet as the covey got up, but I had no clue what was going on. That was the first covey rise I'd ever heard or seen. I knew there were animals moving but I didn't know if it was bears, deer, birds, or even elephants for that matter. I looked up at Uncle Simmons for reassurance.

His eyes were glowing with excitement, as he stood ready for any stragglers, shotgun held tight across his midriff. Still looking into the brush with an accomplished grin stretching ear-to-ear, he asked, "Billy, did you see that covey get up?"

"No sir, but I sure heard it. What's a covey?"

The familiar deep laughter reverberated throughout the trees at the back of the field. "I think they flew into the woods. We can't get them from here. Let's just keep walking around the field," Uncle Simmons suggested, knowing he and Daddy would have waded the ditch and shot them. But today, his partners were a six-year-old and an eleven-year-old, who were ill-equipped for wading or briar-busting.

Immediately readjusted after the excitement of the covey rise, Betty was still talking. She was never captivated as much by the wildlife as Uncle Simmons, nor her budding naturalist brother, but she craved the fatherly companionship and came away from our jaunts as nourished as I. In mid-soliloquy, she spotted some mistletoe sprouting high in a sweet gum and begged Uncle Simmons to shoot it down. He did and we gathered it to hang over the door at Grandmamma's house. I didn't understand its significance and had a hard time figuring out why we were hunting a plant instead of something that flew or ran. But for an eleven-year-old little girl approaching the boy-crazy teen years, it was the highlight of the day for Betty. Brief and rare as they were, we each found our own refuge in these interludes.

After supper that night, I stayed at Granddaddy's house until it grew dark outside. Laid out on the floor and playing with Army men, I was spending time with Uncle Simmons and listening to him talk with Grandmamma and Granddaddy in the front room of their house. Yet, I was not really taking part in the conversation. Like most kids back then, I was mostly playing on the floor and being seen versus being heard. But I was smack-dab in the middle of the family, right where I wanted to be and where they wanted me to be.

Every now and then, Uncle Simmons would wink and playfully kick my foot, or ask a journalistic question about Batman to obligingly get me involved in the conversation, much like he would quiz a senator from Washington D.C.—no doubt, without the kick. He kept me at the precipice of excitement, but if my attentiveness did wane, he'd wink my way or ask to inspect one of my plastic men. And of course, there was always the possibility of his pulling out a new gadget. Uncle Simmons always had a new gadget or something unusual and useful that he could show us. It might be a camping lantern, or a pocketknife, or a new rod, or a hand warmer, or anything—it really didn't matter. Even better, it was usually outdoor-oriented, which to me was like throwing gasoline on the boyhood flames of fidget. Noticing the time, Uncle Simmons leaned forward. "Billy, I have something to show you that I know you will like immensely. Come with me!" While he marched up the wide staircase that led to the room where he and Aunt Ruth always stayed, I waited at the bottom in fitful anticipation.

After zipping zippers and slamming drawers so long I thought daybreak would come any second, Uncle Simmons finally strode downstairs with the absolute longest, shiniest flashlight I'd ever seen. Of course, just like a Washington politician wanting to see his name in a magazine, I decoyed right up. I was just itching to get my hands on that chrome-plated powerful new manly instrument with the gigantic lens.

"You like that, do you?" came the ever-observant rhetorical question, along with his deep chuckle. "Say goodbye to your Granddaddy, Grandmamma, and Ruth and I'll walk you back home. We'll check her out."

Gently closing the screen door behind us and making sure it didn't slam since that would draw fire from Grandmamma, we walked out onto the front porch. Uncle Simmons clicked the button on the flashlight and slowly swung the glowing beam toward the old structure directly across the road that was my great-grandfather's first house. In my youth, we jumped out of its second story window onto hay bales kept there for our cattle. The piercing light carried for what seemed like a mile and lit up the whole house like a WWII air raid. Uncle Simmons shined it up into the far branches of the giant sycamores and over the trunks of the mottled gum trees that framed the old house like bare Halloween skeletons leaning over a ghostly grave.

"You think we can spot a raccoon up there, Billy?" He grinned my way.

At that point in my life, I'd never seen a raccoon and the thought of discovering one of the fanged fugitive creatures peering down at us from every tree fork—snarling its discontent and readying itself to race down and dine upon our carcasses—was mesmerizing. I'd cupped up, plopped down in the decoys, and tipped my tail to feed by then.

"I'm sure your mom wants you home by 8. Let's get rolling, Billy."

Stepping off the porch, we began our slow journey down the single lane rock road. Purposely building to a crescendo the nervous excitement of a six-year-old boy, Uncle Simmons flashed the light up into each and every tree, suggesting that one of the secretive furbearers may be hunching just over the next limb, or crouching around the next trunk. Of course, at six years old, I envisioned all kinds of vicious creatures behind every tree and bush. But somehow, walking with Uncle Simmons, I knew they'd stay where they belonged. My main focus was on the powerful white beam, as it danced amongst the limbs, creating imaginary animal shapes at the dark intersections of every shadow.

"You think he's up there, Billy? Maybe he's in this one?" I can hear him chuckle now, just like I did on that 200-yard expedition. To him, it may have been a few minutes of polite gesturing, good-natured kidding, and probable reflection on times past. For me, it was a mystical walk in nature, after dark, in the cool settling fall air, with the late December stars shimmering above us—alongside a reassuring mentor. And it was preparation for a lifetime of fascination. Upon busting into the kitchen, I immediately told Mom I knew exactly what I now wanted for Christmas.

"And what is that?" she asked, throwing a half-scolding, half-amused glance toward Uncle Simmons.

"A flashlight, just like Uncle Simmons has!" I shouted.

"Oh really?" came Mom's reply. "Well, I'm not sure Santa has the ability to do that right now, but we'll see."

Even at six, I knew, "We'll see" was a grown-up way to say, "Probably not, but let's talk about it later." After I got the familiar rubbing on my crew cut, Mom walked Uncle Simmons to the backdoor, where he left to go back to Granddaddy's house.

I got ready for bed, thinking about the next few days to come and dreaming of long silver flashlights.

Santa didn't bring me a flashlight that year, but Uncle Simmons returned the next Spring, with another gadget ready for me. "Well, looka there. Hey, Billy, I've got something just for you!" he gusted, as I ran up to Grandmamma's house to greet him. He walked to the trunk of his car, reached into his tackle box, and pulled out a hunting knife. Like most boys growing up in the rural South in the 1960s, knives fascinated me. Pocketknives, Barlow knives, hunting knives, butcher knives, Bowie knives, trapper knives, scout knives—it didn't matter. If it was a knife, I wanted it. I wanted to touch them; I wanted to cut with them; I wanted to just look at them. It's hard to describe the affection for outside gear—knives in particular—that I still have today. "Knives and flashlights... you have issues with knives and flashlights," my wife accuses regularly. Her perceptiveness is one of the main reasons I married her; she is usually right on the money.

Uncle Simmons did nothing but incubate, exacerbate and nurture my issues. He slowly slid the Excalibur out of its sheath like a magician pulling a rabbit out of a hat, coyly checking his youthful audience, and building suspense like an unscheduled presidential press conference. It had a glossy black leather handle, brilliant red spacers just above the satin brass finger guard and just below the silver pommel, and a five-inch blade that looked like Jim Bowie's sword to me.

"Billy, I thought maybe it's time for you to have a knife. But now ... uh, you know, we *will* have to talk to your mother." He took it out and handed it to me, and as he looked down with a self-satisfied encouraging possum grin, I felt confident that I'd have an ally in the upcoming fence-walking conversations. Maybe we could complete this sale together? Making sure I didn't touch the blade as directed by Uncle Simmons, I kneaded the hard leather handle and tested the finger guard. I imagined how it would stick solidly into a pine tree and quiver there after I expertly threw it over-handed like Daniel Boone hurled his hatchet or like James West cast the knife he hid discreetly in the back of his jacket. Probably sensing my growing heretical desire to caress the blade, Uncle Simmons took back the knife and headed toward Grandmamma's kitchen. "Hold on now. We've got some work to do here, Billy."

Following loyally behind my new partner in subversion, I glanced toward Grandmamma who was making some buttermilk biscuits. Though she smiled, she turned and looked away, probably knowing there was a storm coming, despite the clear day. Uncle Simmons began to encase the knife with electrical tape, wrapping and re-wrapping the blade, then he re-sheathed it, stepped back, and ordered, "Put it on your belt. Let's see how it looks!"

It's a good thing that belt wasn't any tighter because it would have busted wide open with all the pride swelling me up. That knife looked perfect and felt even better on my hip. Now I could be like some of the older boys around the neighborhood, and God only knows what kind of trouble I could get into!

Wisely, Uncle Simmons suggested we walk over to the store to let Mom know and get her okay. That sounded simple enough. I was excited at the idea of showing Mom, but something in the back of my mind told me that she may not be as excited as I was. I'm not sure what, if any, trepidation Uncle Simmons might have been experiencing. Looking back on it, I'm pretty sure he realized there was going to be some interesting discussion, and he was probably making plans to hightail it back to Grandmamma's after the dreaded announcement.

Mom was standing behind the cash register, as I high-stepped into the store. Her eyes shifted immediately to my belt. Though this was supposed be our mutual journey of explanation, Uncle Simmons had somehow fallen a few steps behind me. I pulled out the taped knife and, to her credit, Mom did not totally destroy a young boy's budding pride in his newfound possession. After a brief show and tell, it was suggested that my Army men left outside next to the store needed to be picked up—right then. Years later, Mom told me about the conversation she had with Uncle Simmons. I don't know exactly how it went but she made it abundantly clear that she did not want me to have a knife, and that Uncle Simmons had just singlehandedly rendered useless a year of careful denials by her. Always the family peacemaker, Mom did eventually let me wear the knife around on my belt, but I had to keep tape on it at all times. It was kind of like having a Milky Way in your pocket, but you could only feel it; you couldn't eat it. It wasn't exactly material for a *Boy's Life* story, and I understood my new knife's inadequacy would be pounced upon by the hawk-like boys of prey in the neighborhood. But as a young negotiator, I took the croaker on the table and figured maybe somehow, a trout would show up later.

When I was in my late teens, Uncle Simmons told me his version of that conversation with Mom. It was pretty close to hers, but while he never said it, I think in his mind a boy needed to walk the edge of safety sometimes, take a little risk, be just a tad dangerous—like when he and his brothers jumped off the diving platform at the drop-off in Bay River. It was part of maleness, part of the fathering he knew my dad would have carried out if he'd been given the chance. It was his way of helping my father. I wish I still had that knife. Instead, it was a victim of a boy's proclivity to misidentify priorities and was probably lost in the woods or thrown out with excess model car parts.

Yes, I have an "issue" with knives, and once in a while, I cut myself both literally and figuratively. But none of the many knives I now own can make up for the absence of that black-handled beauty.

Grandmamma died in 1971 and Granddaddy joined her in 1975. As time passed, my sister and I grew to be teenagers, pursuing our own interests and educations while Uncle Simmons's correspondent duties in Washington kept him very busy. I suppose coming home for him just wasn't the same. But in December of my junior year of high school, he called and asked if he could get in some dove hunting with me. This would be the first time I'd hunt with him when we both carried guns and I was eager to see if this could be a new chapter of a shelved book—albeit composed of changed characters. I was very excited. Though the memories of my early boyhood were distant, they still resonated; it would be great to take the next step. On the way down, Uncle Simmons stopped by Little Washington and picked up my cousin Stevie so he could join us.

That morning dawned bitterly cold and while waiting for Uncle Simmons and Stevie to arrive, I drove up the Alfred Swamp Road to scout. There were quite a few doves coming to a 200-acre field of cut soybeans, but I had doubts that we could effectively shoot them with only three people.

After they arrived and we had lunch, we loaded up, drove to the field and parked. Usually, winter doves may not fly until 2:00 p.m. or so, but that day there were already hundreds feeding in the field, trying to store up energy for the approaching frigid evening. We hurriedly gathered our shells, coats, and guns and rushed to our respective stations about 200 yards apart. Once we got down in the ditches, it didn't take long for the barrage to start. The frantic doves were barreling into that field in steady flocks of five to fifteen birds, one after another, back-to-back, dipping and diving, just a few feet off the ground. I shucked and re-shucked shells into my daddy's Winchester double-barrel shotgun and Stevie tried to keep his automatic filled, while Uncle Simmons expertly and efficiently fed his old Remington Sportsman shotgun. All three guns barked continuously for at least three hours. At sixteen, I was certainly not a great shot, but I'd learned enough to beat down my usual share with a good amount of shooting. But that day, I was so excited and there were so many birds coming so fast and so often that I couldn't have hit anything, even with a 10-gauge punt gun. I don't know how many boxes of shells I went through, but it was the most doves coming to a field I'd ever seen in my life, except for one other time. Stevie shot about the same pace as me, but Uncle Simmons couldn't miss. I remember being surprised at how such a worldly man, who lived and worked in the city and who only sparingly ventured out into the country, could shoot so well. He was knocking them out right and left, high and low, side to side, face on, going away and in every other conceivable direction. At one point, one of his high overhead-shot victims helicoptered out of the air, stone dead. As the bird fell past his head, Uncle Simmons reached out and grabbed it right out of mid-air.

Smiling broadly and whipping adolescent boy envy to a froth, he held the vanquished prize high. Then he ceremoniously stuffed the dove into the game pouch in his jacket. You could hear that deep bellowing laugh reverberate all over Maribel. To a sixteen-year-old boy raised among shotguns and bean fields, that was about as close as you could get to delirium, without involving Charlie's Angels. That entire afternoon, the birds continued to swarm into the field, and we continued to burn powder—unproductively for Stevie and me, but fittingly rewarding for Uncle Simmons. Walking out late in the day, with the orange sun lowering to the west, the temperature rapidly falling and hundreds of doves still flying, I knew it had been special. I thought about that day for many years; the steady streams of birds hastily seeking out much-needed winter feed, Uncle Simmons's boisterous laugh, and how it must have seemed like old times for him. We'd learned from our uncle, and he'd showed us how he used to do it. It was a glimpse of what could have been, had my father lived.

A year and a half later, I graduated from high school, but before leaving for college, a friend of mine and I traveled to Washington, D.C., to see all the sights. I'd never taken the complete tour and Uncle Simmons was excited to host us. We spent several days visiting the Smithsonian, the Archives, and all the monuments and memorials. Uncle Simmons ate dinner with us every night, talked to us about what we'd seen that day and asked us questions. He was very interested in what we'd learned. Always a bit bookish but never to the extent that he conveyed any awkwardness at all, Uncle Simmons appreciated and respected knowledge. He got that from Grandmamma, who'd been a schoolteacher. He wanted to make sure our time in D.C. was educational and enjoyable; indeed, it was both. I learned much about our nation's symbols and history, gaining a unique perspective on many historical and political topics during those evening dinners with Uncle Simmons. We even dropped him off at the Capitol for an interview with a senator one day.

Thirty days after that trip to Washington, I left Maribel for Chapel Hill. As another North Carolinian once alluded, you can never go home again. On that August day in 1978, I certainly had that feeling as I rolled out of that same small rock lane where Uncle Simmons and I walked that starry December night, and where Betty and I used to run to greet him. The assertion that our lives move ahead, and nothing remains the same is indeed true, but on that last day leaving home I nonetheless felt confident that I would have many future memories in the home fields of my boyhood. I relished the thought that some of them would be with Uncle Simmons.

But it was not to be. A virulent form of cancer claimed him in 1981. As he battled, Betty and I wanted to visit Uncle Simmons, but he asked us not to come. I think he wanted us to remember him the way he lived, full of energy, spirit, and humor. He got his wish.

A few years ago, I'd just finished one of the stories in this book and like many aspiring writers, I was interested in perhaps publishing it. Aunt Ruth was one of the first people with whom I shared it. She actually liked the story, and suggested I contact a friend of Uncle Simmons's who still worked with the Raleigh newspaper, so I could get his advice and input.

I contacted the gentleman and subsequently emailed the story to him. He also liked it, offering to discuss it over lunch. As we reviewed the good and not-so-good points of my story, the conversation eventually got around to Uncle Simmons. His father and Uncle Simmons had been very good friends and had a history together working in Raleigh. He shared with me his admiration for Uncle Simmons and told me several old war stories. We laughed at some of my uncle's past humor, agreed on some of his idiosyncrasies and reflected on his interesting career. It was a unique and different perspective on Uncle Simmons's life that I had not known. Toward the end of our lunch, the gentleman shared with me a story I'd never heard before that day. Sometime in the 1970s, he had gone to Washington, D.C., and had stopped by Uncle Simmons's office at *Time*. When he walked into Uncle Simmons's office, he was introduced to two other young men who were also visiting Uncle Simmons. It appeared the two men were friends, and after the initial obligatory hellos and chit chat, those gentlemen soon left. Later, after he returned from Washington, he realized the two men also visiting Uncle Simmons that day were two very famous journalists. Evidently, Uncle Simmons had been friends with both of them. I was astonished that Uncle Simmons had never mentioned this to me, even though he knew I'd followed Washington politics from an early age. He'd covered President Nixon and the White House in the early 1970s and, as a correspondent, had actually flown on Air Force One with Nixon. I knew all about it and feeling a connection to what was happening in Washington, had even watched the Watergate hearings that were a mainstay of daytime TV during the summer of 1973.

Subsequently, I had come to admire our elder Tar Heel statesman and Chairman of the Senate Watergate Committee, Senator Sam Ervin, Jr. When preparing a high school research paper, I had even written Senator Ervin to ask his opinion regarding some key historic attributes of southern politics, and he aptly responded to me with a letter and signed picture. But not crowing about his accomplishments nor his contacts was very typical of Uncle Simmons. He was taught that by Grandmamma, who was never conversational about herself and who undoubtedly instilled that same quality in her children. Uncle Simmons had a wonderful way with people. He would sit down with you and perhaps pat you on the back—not in a disingenuous way, but in a "I'm concerned about you" way. This, combined with his joking personality, allowed most people to relax around him. He concentrated on you and didn't try to dominate a conversation by telling you what he was doing or thinking. He listened.

Too often today in our world of texting and email, these personal subtleties of human interaction are lost in our society.

Instead of realness, many seem content to post representations on the internet of what they appear to be and tell us what they want us to think they are.

Uncle Simmons was more concerned with who you really were. He wanted to sit down with you in person and find out about you. And you felt it. While he loved his work and the myriad friends he'd met through it, I always got the feeling that when he was with me, he enjoyed talking to me, and that he wanted to talk only with me at that precise moment. Whether we looked for coons in the trees or conspired about knives or walked the banks of Bay River, or just talked about hunting, fishing, or the farm, he made me feel like we had a connection. I suspect he did that for others, as well. I often wonder what Uncle Simmons would think about journalism today. It has morphed tremendously since his career began in the smoke-filled typewriter rooms of newspapers in the Southeast. He understood the role of journalism in this country, and I believe he tried to practice it daily. I've read some of his articles and I can tell he tried to be loyal to his patriotic roots and do the right thing while covering, with his passion for fairness, national stories in the era of Vietnam, social discontent, and political scandals.

Twenty years ago, Uncle Simmons was inducted into the North Carolina Journalism Hall of Fame. My sister and I planned to attend along with Aunt Ruth, but at the last minute, Aunt Ruth got sick and couldn't make the trip from Washington to Chapel Hill. She called and asked if I could accept the award on her behalf. I told her I certainly would and that it would be an honor.

As I drove up that evening, I debated what to say but soon decided. An old public speaking mentor of mine told me once, "When in doubt, be brief." So, I efficiently thanked the nominating committee, the attendees and all involved and accepted on behalf of Uncle Simmons, Aunt Ruth and our families. I told them I knew he loved his work and took great pride in it. But I also briefly described how my sister and I spent time with him when we were growing up and how that was as important to us as any of his professional accomplishments. I thought it was fitting that they see the other side of him.

Aunt Ruth passed away a few years ago but before she died, my wife, daughter, and I visited her in Chevy Chase. One evening after dinner, she led me downstairs to the basement, reached in a closet and pulled out the old Remington Sportsman. There was a worn, oil-stained rag wrapped around the action, no doubt put there after being cleaned by Uncle Simmons—perhaps after our memorable dove hunt.

"Billy, I want you to have this. Simmons would want you to have it," she offered, knowing it would have a safe and appropriate home. With a humble spirit and memories flooding back, I accepted. At the time of its purchase in the late 1950s, the relatively unadorned working man's shotgun was marketed as a budget-minded alternative to the finer Brownings. It is in my gun safe now, taking its esteemed position at the rear with a note tied to it, so my daughter will one day know its history. And it's worth a fortune to me. Maybe this fall when the weather turns, I'll get the old gun out, corral my daughter, pile into the truck and head up the Alfred Swamp Road with our dog, Beau. Hopefully, we'll see some doves, or maybe we'll hear a bobwhite. Perhaps, she'll want me to shoot down some mistletoe for the front door. I'll make the time.

Thanksgiving at Granddaddy's

Just when the world seems intolerable, the country is on the brink and upside down and most people seem to be pre-occupied with unimportant humanistic substitutes for what is really important, God has a way of sending us a message. As I returned from the post office the day before Thanksgiving, and in the midst of contemplating current budgetary issues—both professional and personal—I glanced at the pecan trees bordering the parking lot behind my office. Suddenly, I thought back to the preceding October, when summoned by a scolding bushytail, I had ventured over to the patch of woods just west of where I park. Peering up into the two pecan trees that day, it was evident to me that 2020 had not only been a bumper year for chaos, it had been more importantly a tremendous mast year. The trees were full of pecans, just waiting to be plucked and hurled to the ground by the first gales of November. I had made a mental note that day... which had promptly gone the same path as anything else I don't write down these days. Until that Wednesday.

Shouldering all the concerns of a typical business day and intermittently contemplating the consequences of a venison-less freezer hanging over my head, I took a break and walked over to the patch of ground just under the pecan trees. Carefully inspecting the dry leaves for the slightest clue of a light-brown little morsel, I spotted my first two. Almost as excited as the squirrel that was barking off to my left, I promptly scooped them up and automatically arranged them in my right hand at just the right angles, so I could crack one against the other. It's kind of like riding a bike—you don't forget how to do that. You've got to be firm, but not brutal. Not too hard, not too light. Just enough to crack around the whole shell. I've done it in my chair, my boyhood yard, hunting camps, duck blinds, dove fields, trailing behind Mack and Missy Thanksgiving week while laughing with my quail hunting buds, and walking around Granddaddy's yard. Right on cue, the familiar roundness I felt in my hands as I held them, and the first crack, flooded me with memories of Thanksgiving in Alliance with Granddaddy Mayo.

Those were highlights of the 1960s and early 1970s—full of aunts, uncles, and cousins, turkey, dressing, sweet potato casserole, bear meat, venison, fruit Jell-O—the kind that looks like a bunch of pirate jewels suspended in frozen cherry Kool-Aid—gravy boats, homemade biscuits, chocolate cake, ice cream and myriad other scrumptious fare. After we were through with the traditional feast, the dishes were done and cut-up cigars smoked in pipes, we all went outside into the cold November sunshine (it was never seventy-five degrees back then) with Granddaddy and searched under his three trees for pecans. The whole family participated although the grown-ups sort of lollygagged. But for some of us, especially me as the baby of the group, it was serious business. I would even venture into the chicken pen where the little brown prizes were scattered among other gray, not-so-sought-after landmines. But if you were careful and observant with a keen eye like Granddaddy taught me to be with his single shot .22, a boy could come out of there with a handful.

At first, all of us cousins huddled close to Granddaddy as we scanned the ground, then eventually scattered among ourselves to find the last of the fall delights. It was a big deal to find a pecan, hold it up for parental affirmation, then move on to the next search. It became less important as we grew older. Time passed and those Thanksgivings kind of withered away. The families grew and some of the cousins had children of their own. Life happened.

But that Wednesday before Thanksgiving, as I stopped in the whirlwind and got me a mess of *pee-cans* (not puh-conns), I thought back to those days—of Granddaddy in his white shirt and vest, of Uncle Alfred, Uncle Hallet, Aunt Mary and Mom all walking around the yard where they grew up. To them, it must have been like going back in time. It's important to do that sometimes.

・・・

That night, Susan was preparing her mother's sweet potato casserole recipe while I cracked pecans and told her about my day in the parking lot. The high-priced store-bought pecans she sprinkled on top were delicious the next day, but they weren't rolled around in my hands like those from behind my office, or like the ones from a cold Alliance yard many years ago. And they didn't have Mayo flavor added.

Mack

Mack was tired and cold. He never knew how cold these March nights could get outside of his doghouse the Man built just before quail season when he was seven years old. But after spending all of these nights alone in the woods, the English setter now knew. He also knew what it meant to be hungry and confused. He hadn't eaten a full meal or seen the Man for a long time. He didn't know how long it had been, but he knew it was getting harder to remember that last hunting day on the farm with the Man. He still didn't understand exactly what had happened that day.

After following and pointing the single bird that had flushed and flown across the creek, Mack had realized that the Man hadn't followed him. Usually, the Man was close behind when Mack decided to take out on some rambling excursion directed by that wet black independent organ at the end of his snout. He'd held that point for a long time, just like the Man had trained him to do. But still, the Man had not come. Eventually, the bird flushed and Mack broke point to return to where the Man usually parked the familiar green pickup with the dog box in the back. But the Man was not there.

Mack had looked for the Man a long time, roaming back and forth across the farm until he'd finally given up and bedded down in the woods. Each and every day since, he'd looked for the Man in all the old places, with no success.

Now, as another night closed in and the pains in Mack's stomach started to become even more noticeable, he remembered the warmth and contentment he always felt after the meals the Man used to give him. He thought of the clang of that tin garbage can being opened in the garage back home; that was where the Man kept his food. That was a welcome, exciting sound and very different from the clinking noise made by the empty discarded cans of human food Mack now scattered around the dump while searching for any small bit of nourishment to help him make it through one more night. The opening of the garbage can always made him shake with excitement. Tonight, he shook from cold and hunger. He wished he could hear that familiar clang announcing the old feed time. He wanted to feel the routine pat on top of his head and hear the Man's soothing voice while he ate, like he'd felt and heard so many times since he first came home as a one-year-old puppy in 1988. Mack wondered if he would ever feel that pat or hear the Man's reassuring voice again.

That first Saturday in February of 2001 had dawned pleasant enough in eastern North Carolina with gray skies, the temperature in the low fifties and no wind. It was not a perfect quail hunting day, but a day good enough to take my fourteen-year-old, slightly deaf setter, Mack, and ten-year-old precocious pointer, Missy, down to the family farm to at least walk some ditch banks and relive old times. Besides, I wanted my fiancée, Susan, to see what bird hunting was all about. She had already obligingly accompanied me into a beaver pond that winter, experiencing mallards landing within feet of where she sat motionless. Although she'd passed that test, she hadn't seen what truly stirred her soon-to-be-husband's soul. She hadn't seen what I wanted her to see: white tails held straight and high with eager brown eyes searching a tangled hedgerow for any signs of movement. She had not witnessed my rust-ticked setter and liver-splotched pointer trembling in anticipation of a final uproar, that culminating moment when nine, ten, or twelve birds erupt skyward; when the choreography of dogs, the whirring of exploding wings, the flashes of brown, russet and white and the sure movement of the shotguns and the smell of powder, all come together to create a perfect ten seconds in time. She had not seen in person the story told by albums of pictures I'd accumulated over the previous thirteen years. But with us three other hunters eager to accept her into our private world that only quail hunters truly know, we left home and headed to the farm that Saturday—Susan and I, Mack, and Missy, all following a February Saturday tradition genetically transferred from my father, and from Mack's sire and dam and Missy's sire and dam.

This tradition of southern bird hunting is uniquely comprised of its own grace and etiquette. It's a passion that is deeply rooted in the bonds between hunters and well-trained dogs, and in a reverence for clear fall afternoons filled with vivid colors, loblolly pines, stiff tan canvas coats, standing soybeans, and the brown birds to whom it is all dedicated. Like my father and stepfather, I have a passion for the sport. Amidst couple's conversation during the two-hour drive to the farm, I thought about those traditions of the sport and the stories of twenty-five-bird days told to me by my stepfather, Alf, and memories of my own eight-bird and six-bird hunts that were just as special to me. I thought about my father and how at my age then of forty-one, he was stricken with cancer during the last days of bird season in February 1961. I thought about how he must have felt lying in the hospital with a one-year-old boy back home, knowing he would never share these beloved afternoons with me. I wished I could have hunted with my father and that he could have seen Mack in his prime and Missy busting a covey like she was prone to do. And I wished he could have met my fiancée.

• • •

We arrived at the farm and the ritual began. I walked around to the back of the truck, barely able to hear Susan ask if it was time to put on her boots over the cacophony of whining, barking, yelping and tails being violently hurled against the aluminum dog box—all demanding release from the last obstacle preventing Mack and Missy from doing what they were bred to do, and indeed commanded to do by instinct—hunt for the bobwhite. Standing aside so as not to lose an appendage or at the very least, be knocked completely unconscious, I opened the doors of the dogbox and let them go. And they went. First to take care of the usual canine business, then to sniff, scratch, run, and bark with excitement as they tried to determine from my slightest movement where we would go this time. With a frantic lack of patience, they watched as I tied my cracked leather boots, zipped up the torn orange vest, looped the whistle around my neck and uncased the Winchester Model 24 double-barrel with bluing worn to a silvery shine, a tribute to the half century of use, first by my father and then by me.

As I broke the gun down to load, I motioned with a hand for them to be off; we'd head to Marvin's hedgerow first today. The line of trees at the back of the farm was so named about ten years earlier when my hunting partner and friend, Marvin, had missed a "few" shots as birds flushed from the hedgerow on a brilliant Thanksgiving morning. A "few" was defined by me as, "A minimum of ten that Mack had never more finely pointed and that flew Marvin's direction because of the obvious safety in doing so."

It was defined by Marvin as, "Probably three that happened to jump up wild in front of an out-of-control dog." Regardless of the reasons, it was called Marvin's hedgerow from then on. Anyway, Mack and Missy knew it well. They knew that today with a northwest wind, we would start at the east end and head west while staying on the south side. They even seemed to understand that today Susan would walk with us on the leeward side instead of on the windward side of the hedgerow, the usual assigned position for guests. But we all knew that if birds were found, it would be my fault when they all flew out the side where nobody could shoot. So be it. Today was a day to enjoy, to reflect on years gone by and to introduce the new girl to the sport—to the sanctity of it all. The first couple of hours proved to be unproductive, as far as birds were concerned. This wasn't surprising since our number of bagged birds had declined over the last few years. This decrease in harvest was directly related to several well-known hedgerows being cut down so that the local farmers could gain productivity and to less available cutovers in that two-to-five-year growth stage that offers both find-ability and shoot-ability of Mr. Bob. Of course, it was just possible that some of the reduction in the numbers of quail ending up in brown gravy may have been associated with the progressing age of the three hunters and even with my slight realigning of priorities toward the increasing duck populations and limits. Whatever the reasons, we had no birds. But at the same time, we weren't concerned or disappointed. The dogs were happy, with tails whipping and noses flaring; every hole, bush, and cranny was being inspected, the air was filled with the combined scent of harvest residue and brown winter earth—and we were initiating a new convert. It was a good day to be alive, and as our entire group turned at the end of the field and headed south making a loop to the hardwoods at the back of the farm, we knew it. There was a possibility that we might even find that covey near the creek. There had always been a shy covey that took refuge beside the creek at the back of the hardwoods on the west end of the farm. Despite the fact that this covey hadn't even been seen in five years, I thought the mixed woods of oaks and pine would render a nice break in terrain for the dogs and a pleasant walk for Susan and me. Besides, I could proudly show Susan the loblolly pine, where at twelve years old in the fall of 1972, I shot my first squirrel with the Model 24, probably not far from where my father had killed his first quail with the same gun. I could also point out the gigantic white oak under which I'd been sitting when three does walked within ten feet on a frosty October morning in 1973, forever searing into my memory that excitement that only comes from being so close to animals that you can see the wildness in their eyes and hear the air escape from their lungs. There was also the old cow wallow where I'd seen my first bear track at fourteen, and the headwaters where I'd seen a pair of nesting wood ducks when such a sight was not that common. I had grown up on our family farm and in the woods adjacent to it, and I wanted to share it all with her. Out front, Mack and Missy worked back and forth through the woods, examining likely smells with scientific precision, while totally dismissing others into that world of unimportant non-birdy stuff. As usual, they checked back regularly by running up, obtaining the needed approval, and then moving on to continue their mission. There was hurried excitement when Mack got birdy near a tangle of briars next to some palmettos. He was right at the edge of the creek, near where he'd pointed the woods covey ten years earlier, when a friend and I had, upon a tight covey rise, shot two birds, one of which fell across the creek. Though ten years had passed, I could tell by the spirit in Mack's eyes that he too recalled that this place held special memories. Deep in his bird dog mind he remembered "The Retrieve."

I referred to it as, "The Retrieve" because at the sound of the guns that day, Mack had immediately picked out the far bird falling across the creek, catapulted himself into the tea-stained water, swam across, gone straight to the bird, brought it back to the far creekbank, jumped in like a champion Lab and swam back to the near bank, depositing the quail gently into my hand as he crawled out and shook. At the time, Mack had acted nonchalant, though he knew I was as proud as I'd ever been, as evidenced by my shouting of "That's my boy" and my high-fiving with my friend. But Mack had been pleased with himself, too, and I knew it. It was apparent by the confident way he had held his head, the same way he'd held it when he'd done something right in training as a one-year-old puppy. We always had that kind of communication, the type that made me believe he remembered that day a decade ago. We were a team, solidified over the last thirteen years.

Now, I waited and watched respectfully as my aging partner searched the creek bank thoroughly. This time, he decided it held no birds. Then, he started to climb up the bank to rejoin the group. He'd done the same thing many times. Yet, this time, his old bones and weakened muscles wouldn't allow him to pull himself back onto the bank. He tried several times, but he just couldn't do it anymore. He looked at me with a bewildered expression that struck a chord deep within me. After all these years, his once strong body was now showing its frailty. I hesitated and could only look at him for a moment. But Susan reached down, whispered something in his ear and helped him back up. He liked her. Things had changed for Mack and me, but that was okay. Ten years ago, we would have hunted another three hours until dark; today, we were turning to go back to the truck. Missy was at our side, and as we came out of the woods, Susan asked, "Have you seen Mack?"

"No, I haven't," I replied.

Then again, that wasn't unusual. Mack had always tended to wander off for five minutes, maybe ten, especially when there were no birds. The dogs hadn't been out in a while, and they were anxious. Even at fourteen, and tiring after a couple of hours in the field, Mack was a headstrong dog and he had probably decided to go a short distance on his own.

"I'm sure he'll show up in a couple of minutes," I reassured her.

Missy jumped into the back of the truck and took her usual seat in the dog box, waiting for the next stop. The Model 24 was put away in the old canvas case and the vest placed behind the dog box. As I turned and glanced toward the woods, I fully expected to see the setter ambling back to the truck in that side-saddle gait that I'd seen so many times, the kind of sideways jog that resembles one of those vehicles you see on the road that's been hit so hard in a previous accident that its chassis has been bent and although the front wheels are coming right at you, the rear wheels are aimed amusingly to one side. Mack had possessed that gate since he was a puppy. But as I scanned from the woods to the field to the hedgerow, blowing the whistle, yelling my buddy's name, I did not see that familiar gait; I saw no sign of Mack. It had been thirty minutes since we'd last seen him, since Susan had pulled Mack out of the creek and the setter had checked in one last time. I continued to blow the whistle as thirty minutes turned into forty-five minutes and slight puzzlement as to Mack's location changed to concern. It was now 4:00 p.m. and it would be dark in less than two hours. Susan and I hurried through the woods, across the fields and up and down the hedgerows searching every spot that a rogue bird jumped by Mack could have flown and, thus, where Mack might be found still hunting some shadowy scent that remained strong enough for further investigation, simultaneously providing the setter an excuse not to return to the pickup. We both yelled his name and blew the whistle, knowing Mack could not hear very well. Of course, at times he could hear just fine, like when I opened the garbage can in the garage to get the food out for the nightly feed. I thought of that and how Mack's convenient hearing reminded me of what Mom used to say about Granddaddy: that he could sometimes hear exactly what he wanted to hear. So, I kept blowing the whistle and we both kept calling his name, hoping that by now Mack wanted to hear the whistle and his name. But my confidence that we'd find Mack—at first, bolstered by the memory of several instances when he had temporarily disappeared and then returned after some period of time uniquely defined by Mack as ample—waned as we completed the loop of the farm. As a child, and even as an adult, I'd read in many magazines how people who had temporarily lost dogs overnight left articles of clothing in the field, so the dog would find the familiar scent and stay there until picked up the next day. While Susan continued to call Mack from beside the truck, I took the orange vest and laid it neatly on the ground, explaining to her that Mack would surely, eventually backtrack and come to this familiar site. He'd then find the vest and hunker down for a comfortable, if somewhat cool, night out, knowing that I would be back the next day to pick him up. Even as I recited this bit of universally accepted outdoor lore, there was a growing sense of dread. Mack was fourteen years old, deaf, and not as strong as he used to be. I knew that some dogs preferred to die alone, and it was at least a possibility that Mack was out there by himself, dying or already dead. But I put that thought out of my mind and, as we made a final swing through all the farm roads within two miles of the woods where Mack was last seen, I tried to remain optimistic.

Later, we stopped at Alf's house and told him about Mack. I asked him to phone us if anyone called his house. Most everyone in the area knew me and although my home phone number was on the collar, someone might first call Alf. Reluctantly, but slightly encouraged by the knowledge that we'd be back in the morning, we left to go back home.

Susan and I were up Sunday morning before dawn and arrived at the farm just after 8:00 a.m. We drove immediately to the place where the vest had been placed the day before, but Mack was nowhere to be found. We'd both hoped that Mack would be there waiting for us, but now reality began to sink in.

We searched the same fields and woods that we'd covered on Saturday, calling and blowing the whistle. We drove around all the local farms several times, scouring the fields with binoculars. Mack was nowhere. We saw tracks but the tracks always disappeared or were obviously too old to be Mack's tracks. We searched the woods behind some houses, thinking maybe Mack had ventured into those yards after smelling table scraps. Every base was covered, every known suspected location that Mack could go was searched—but to no avail.

Morning gave way to afternoon and a light rain began to fall. Susan and I both agreed to make one more pass through the woods, where we'd last seen Mack. As Susan walked through the woods calling Mack's name, I quietly walked the creekbank, dreading the site I almost expected to see; the site of my hunting buddy floating in the creek after not being able to make it back up. But I did not see Mack. Neither of us saw Mack, nor any sign of him. The rain set in, we both became soaked and our expectations that had been so high that morning began to fade. Susan tentatively interjected short, positive assertions such as, "I bet we find him just around this corner," and "I'm sure he's probably back at the truck by now."

But when we arrived at the truck and I saw the undisturbed, wet orange vest, I admitted to myself for the first time that Mack might be gone. I stood there in the rain beside the truck for several minutes, staring back at the woods and the fields, hoping for one last glimpse. Then I looked at Susan, thankful for the rain that disguised the emotion in my eyes. I'd take a vacation day and return the next day, but I didn't expect to find Mack.

That Monday was cool and filled with sunshine and a perfect Carolina-blue sky that contrasted sharply with the brown leafless trees. The robins were chirping everywhere, their red breasts flashing intermittently with their dull gray backs, as whole flocks flew between the hedgerows and the fields. Winter was surely here but robins in the field always meant that spring days were just around the corner. Late season heavy-feathered doves flew their normal routes between the farms, signaling it would not be long before they would be pairing up for the repeated courtship of spring and summer. It was one of those February days in North Carolina that exudes life: crisp, fresh and full of hope for the new seasons coming. I'd spent many such February days with Mack in pursuit of the large year-end coveys that come together when small, ravaged groups of birds unite with others to survive the remaining cold nights of winter.

I searched from sunrise to sunset Monday, trying to take in the gorgeous day and use it as a prop to assure myself that there would be a fruitful end to this, the second day since Mack had been lost. But leaving the farm that night, after Alf and I had put out food just in case Mack showed up at the vest, I'd concluded that Mack was probably dead.

The drive home was long, and my mind drifted back to the day I saw Mack point for the first time. It was ironically a point over scent left by a very nice buck that jumped up in front of me and the breeder who was showing his wares on a fall morning in 1988. I'd liked Mack as soon as I'd seen him. He had a strong athletic build, a beautiful shiny rust and white coat and vibrant amber eyes. He was what the older hunters I'd grown up around called a "classy" dog. Despite my determination not to show too much interest when I first saw Mack at the kennel, the experienced breeder undoubtedly picked up right away on my preference because Mack's price was significantly more than the other dogs and his demonstration was saved for last. And what a demonstration it was.

Mack covered ground easily with a determination unmatched by any of the breeder's other dogs, or by any other I'd ever hunted. He was quick, agile, and graceful. When he got a snoot-full of that buck, he slammed into a rock-solid point and his white feathery tail shot straight up. As he strained his head forward and settled into a slight crouch, his tail continued to tense and slowly rise that last quarter of the way to the eventual 90-degree angle. It was a magnificent example of hundreds of years of work by generations of enthusiasts determined to keep bloodlines pure and maintain traditions, so hunters like me could forever enjoy the beauty of the sport. That might have been the first bird dog ever sold after pointing a deer, but I'd never regretted the purchase. I worked hard to train Mack those first two years, spending many Saturdays shooting pen-raised birds. There were many rides back and forth to the farm with Mack in the back seat of my Blazer, stretching forward to lay his head on my shoulder, confirming his place with me after long Saturdays of hunting.

I remembered how Mack and I had hunted doves up and down the hedgerows during the big Christmas snowstorm of 1989, despite Mom's half-hearted proclamation that no hunters should be out in that blizzard. But I knew Mom understood the thrill I got from roaming the family farm with a good bird dog. She'd seen it before. That day, Mack had instinctively flushed doves from the same hedgerows where we had previously shot quail, enabling me to shoot a limit in one hour, as the birds hurriedly tried to get out of the blizzard and back to the cover. He was a quail dog's quail dog, but that was one day when it had been okay to shoot and retrieve doves.

I thought of many other days afield with my buddy, including the November day in 1995, when Marvin and I started with three wood ducks taken near a beaver dam just before sunrise and just before hearing a surprise covey's single winter whistle reveal its presence less than 300 yards away. We'd finished that day by taking pictures of Mack, Missy, fourteen quail and three wood ducks on the back of the truck with a beautiful red November sunset providing the lighting. Marvin and I had both known there would never be enough of those days. I remembered how Mack had found an unsuspecting covey way out in the middle of a bean field as my friend, Richard, and I doubted there would be any birds that far from cover right up to very minute they flushed, fifty yards from the nearest woods. We followed Richard's dog, Mack, and Missy straight through the middle of that field, with Mack stylishly pointing at the lead, then backing the other dogs, proudly defying his eleven years. We took pictures that day, too, with Mack, Missy and Richard's dog and another bag of fourteen quail.

I remembered how my mother loved Mack and how Mack had reminded her of bird dog puppies she'd raised with my father in the 1950s. I remembered my last conversation with Mom the night before she died just two years earlier, and how my repeated attempts to focus the conversation on the results of her doctor's appointment that day were interrupted by her overwhelming concern for Mack who had recently been sick.

All those memories came back during the drive and, as I arrived home, I hugged Susan a very long time in the doorway.

I searched the farm two more days and, after much thought, logically decided—though I did not accept—that Mack was gone—an elderly dog who had wandered off to die alone.

Three weeks passed and there was no word. The local farmers were notified by Alf and I placed an ad in the local paper. I missed Mack a lot. It was tough coming home every afternoon and not seeing him there in the pen, wagging his tail and looking toward the truck with that wide smile on his face. Mack had been a terrific hunting dog, but he'd also been a loyal and devoted pet. And I wasn't the only one who missed him. Missy moped around for at least two weeks until she finally decided to enjoy her newfound hierarchical status. I eventually got back to the daily grind of work and married the girl of my dreams on February 24, the same day the yellow Lab puppy was born.

At the urging of my new wife, I began entertaining the possibility of getting a Lab puppy. After all, I was duck hunting often now and having some success. I'd always wanted a Lab but could not justify three dogs. But I only owned one dog now and Missy needed company. Yes, now was probably the time, so when an ad appeared in the Raleigh paper expounding the virtues of a certain litter, and that litter was born on our wedding day, I took it to be an indisputable sign that I should answer it.

As soon as I saw the puppy, I knew I'd buy it. After two visits with the owner, I arranged to make the down payment on a Friday, six weeks after the puppy was born—one month and three weeks after Mack was lost.

That Friday morning, I met with the puppy's owner, wrote him a check, and agreed the puppy would be picked up in two weeks. Driving back to the office, I felt excited about the future with the new puppy and the chance to train another dog. I hoped the new puppy would be half as good as Mack. Then I checked my voicemail. A farmer back home had left a message. He'd seen a setter in the field near where Mack had been lost! A peace came over me. If it was Mack, I would be able to finally bury him on the farm and bring the whole tragic event to a proper end. I called the farmer from the truck.

"I got your message," I told the farmer, "and I appreciate your calling."

"Didn't you lose your setter a few weeks ago?" the farmer asked.

"Yessir," I replied.

"Well, I saw a white and brown setter this morning in the wheat field by the old dump, up the swamp road behind your farm. He had a green collar on him. Does that sound like him?"

"Yes, it does," I replied, knowing now I would take the afternoon off to bury my old friend. "Whereabouts in the field is he laying?" I asked.

"He's not laying in the field. He was standing in the field by the dump. He looks real skinny."

I felt a rush of emotion, as I retraced those last words in my mind. "Standing? Skinny?" My mind raced. "You mean he's alive!" I exclaimed.

"Yeah, he's alive," the farmer answered. "He's skinny, but he looks okay."

I pulled off the road to make sure I was hearing correctly. I couldn't believe it. It had been almost two months, and I'd thought Mack was dead—even as I'd begun the conversation with the farmer. Now, to know he was alive was just incredible! "Thank you! Thanks a lot! I'm coming down right now!"

I called my assistant at work and told her that I'd be gone the rest of the day. I'd found my dog and work could wait! Speeding home to change clothes and get the dog box, I called Susan to tell her the unbelievable news. I then called Alf to tell him.

Alf volunteered to drive to the location where Mack was last seen to hopefully pick him up or at least make absolutely sure it was Mack. He called back in thirty minutes, as I was preparing to leave for the farm. "It's Mack," he confirmed. "He's real thin, but it's him. He won't come to me, though. He's mighty skittish. Are you coming on?"

I drove way too fast to the farm, trying to come up with a story that was more believable than, "I'm going to get my dog that's been missing for two months." No highway patrolman would believe that. As it turned out, I didn't get a ticket and arrived at the farm in record time. I went immediately to the area around the dump, parked the truck and began calling and whistling. No Mack. For four hours, I searched everywhere: the woods, the fields, and the hedgerows. I called, whistled and retraced steps I'd made only minutes before. But still, I didn't find my buddy and it was getting dark. One more time, I searched the whole area, then drove all the nearby farm roads. No Mack. I reluctantly got the feed dish from the back of the truck, filled it with dog food and put it down on the grass where Mack had been seen last. Disappointed, I crawled into the truck to drive to Alf's house. I planned to return first thing in the morning to continue the search. As I drove away, I took one last wishful glance in the rearview mirror, but I only saw the pan of food. Alf greeted me at the back door. "Did you get him?" came the anxious question. Now eighty, Alf had been a quail hunter, too. He'd hunted the same fields that I had hunted with Mack. He'd even hunted them with my father many times. He knew all too well the tie between a man and his dog. He had lost his last bird dog, Susie, in 1984 when she was thirteen, and had decided not to get another. It had been the first time in sixty years he hadn't had a bird dog, but he and Mom didn't want to get another dog. They just didn't want to lose another one. So, when I brought Mack home four years later, the rust-ticked setter was adopted by Mom and Alf as their own.

"No, I couldn't find him. I looked all over but I just couldn't find him. I don't know. I thought I would have found him by now.

I'll get up first thing in the morning and start again. You want to go get something to eat?"

"Well, I'm sorry," Alf replied. "I thought you would have had him by now, too. Yeah, I'll ride with you."

We left the house, neither one particularly hungry.

As we approached the dark swamp road that led to where Mack had last been seen, I suddenly turned right and headed toward the dump where I'd left the food only thirty minutes before. Something made me want to try one more time before giving up for the night. *Maybe Mack found the food? Probably not.* But I had a feeling I just needed to go back and not wait until the morning. We pulled into the small road by the dump and my anticipation was high, as the headlights swung around to reveal the pan of food—but nothing else. I slumped down in my seat, disappointed yet again. Alf and I just sat there motionless for a moment.

"Back up a minute," Alf said, as he looked out the passenger window. "There's Mack. He's right there in the grass beside the road!"

"Stay there. Let me get out and go around," I blurted. I didn't want to take any chance that Mack would bolt. Exhilarated, I rushed out the driver side door, ran around the back of the truck and saw him. *Yes, it's Mack*! He was skinny, and slinking off at a quick pace, but it was Mack. I rushed after him, calling his name.

Mack was tired, both physically and mentally. The cold nights and lack of food had taken their toll, but he'd managed to cope with that pretty well. It was the loneliness that had nearly killed him. He missed the gentle rubbing of his ears and the rough play and the whispers of appreciation the Man used to give him. He remembered that new girl had been nice, too. She'd even pulled him out of the creek that last day. He missed all of that, and he missed the nice human voices. He'd only heard gruff voices since that day in February, voices usually screaming at him from a porch as he tried to sneak some scraps. And now there was another man coming at him, yelling something his deaf ears just couldn't understand. But as Mack tired and his pace slowed and the man got closer, he noticed something. That tall, dark, stocky figure moved in familiar ways. Mack hesitated for a moment and turned slightly. He could hear the man yelling something. What was that he was hearing? It sounded like something he knew but just couldn't make total sense of it, like when he was being trained.

He thought back to when he was a puppy and was learning all those commands. Steady. Whoa. Com-eh. During his long training with the Man and, until he had fully learned those commands, he would have vague recollections of what they meant. Then one day, it all clicked, and he'd arrived as a bird dog and knew it.

At that very instant, it clicked again with Mack. He stopped and swung around. It was him! It was the Man! Finally, he'd come back! Once again, Mack felt all those lost puppy feelings that he hadn't felt in years; the kind of all-body excitement that used to come on him suddenly and make him jump off the ground with all four feet; the kind of ecstasy that he always felt when the Man came home at the end of each day.

He wagged his tail uncontrollably, as he hurried to the Man. Burying his nose in the Man's chest, he reveled in the smell of the familiar flannel shirt, jeans, and the tan hunting coat that he knew so well. An overwhelming feeling of relief swept over him and the warmth and contentment he'd missed so much flooded his entire body. It would all be okay now.

I knelt and embraced my buddy. I was forty-one years old, but tears welled up inside of me that I couldn't control. Silent and thankful, I just took a knee beside Mack for a few minutes, petting him, hugging him, rubbing his ears and talking softly to him, thanking God for the gift I had just received. My buddy was home where he belonged; he knew it and I knew it. As I wiped my cheeks and led Mack back to the truck, I noticed Alf putting away his handkerchief. Mack was special to all of us. I lifted Mack into the dog box and headed out. Dropping Alf off at the house, I thanked him and told him that I wanted to go ahead and get Mack back home and get him fed. As I left Alf's house, I called Susan. "I got him!" I shouted. "He's skin and bones, but he's okay. We'll be home in a couple of hours. I love you!"

Just up the road, Mack and I stopped at the local fast-food place. The order was two roast beef sandwiches for Mack and a large diet drink and a cheeseburger for me. Mack got his coming-home feed right there in the parking lot; he even got most of my cheeseburger. Then my dog settled down in his dog box filled with wheat straw for the long ride back to his home. As I drove home that night, I thought about the previous thirteen years: the many steady points, the fourteen-quail days, the high white feathery tails, the great retrieves, the clear blue eastern North Carolina skies, the ambers, reds and browns of the November fields and how magnificent Mack always looked when he was locked up on point with the late fall afternoon sun angling off his white coat. I thought about how the companionship of a once-in-a-lifetime dog had helped me understand my father's and stepfather's love of the gentleman's sport. I thought about how walking the farm with Mack on a March morning in 1999 had helped me through my mother's death and how the setter had welcomed my new wife into our family. Mack was a lucky dog to be found, but I was even more fortunate to have found him.

The Yellow Honeysuckle is the Sweetest

That Friday, Susan was so busy packing for her girls' high school reunion trip to the beach, that it was extra hard to get my usual rise out of her—something I take more than an occasional perverse joy in doing. Finally, I let both barrels fly and challenged her. "I'll tell you what, I'll give $100 to any one of you girls that can tell me five things anybody else said over the entire weekend."

She stopped her feverish packing just long enough to leer back at me. "Oh, now that's rich," she countered. "I'm sure when you're at the hunting club, you know exactly what all the other guys are saying since all of you are just sitting there with everyone listening soooooo intently to each other? Yeah right."

"Most definitely," I agreed.

After confirming the time Sarah got out of pre-school, I told my bride that I loved her and that I hoped she and the other girls had a great time, kissed her goodbye, and waved as she drove away. She was off on her trip, and I was beginning to plan the upcoming father/daughter weekend with our four-year-old little girl.

First, Sarah would play in the evening T-ball game, then we'd eat dinner at home and, after watching *Little Bear*, I'd give her a bath and put her to bed. Saturday morning, we'd get up at our usual 5:30 a.m., eat breakfast, then head down to the "Store" in the Pamlico County to work on the fence, fix the woodshed, throw the Barbie ball, play on the swing, watch cartoons, throw retrieving dummies for Luke, and maybe even catch minnows out of the ditches with the dip net.

According to Sarah, she and I always have a good time at the "Store."

The "Store" is my grandfather's old country store near our farm in Pamlico County, where I grew up. We closed it in 1972, as convenience stores sprung up and Granddaddy aged. Susan and I had recently renovated the old masonry structure, transforming it into a hunting camp and weekend getaway for our family. After a local builder confirmed that it was structurally sound, and with the help of friends, we put on a new red tin roof and installed new windows and doors. New masonry work was completed and new ceiling fans, paneling, propane heaters and a woodstove were installed. The interior was repainted and reconfigured to include two bedrooms, a bathroom, den, and a dining area. It was meticulously furnished with antique family furniture, black and white family pictures, hunting mounts and all kinds of memorabilia—including an old two-man crosscut saw my step-grandfather had owned, and oyster tongs he'd made. Some of the tools and implements are over 100 years old. One item that holds much importance for me probably goes unnoticed by most of our guests. It is a beat-up eight-foot two-by-four broken at one end. When I began the process of cleaning out all the junk in the Store, I found this board under a mangled pile of wet drywall, dirt, discarded furniture and an old door. As soon as I saw it, I knew what it was—despite it being covered with a thick layer of dust. As a boy, I'd spent many hours in the Store, helping Mom and Granddaddy. It was my job to lock the double doors at the front entrance when we closed for the evening. This consisted of hanging a worn, brown, broken board into metal braces on either side of the double doors, so that it stretched across the entrance, effectively preventing anyone from opening the doors by pushing them in. During the day, when the store was open, that broke-end two-by-four was always propped beside the front doors. Because locking the doors was my responsibility, I touched that board almost every day. To me, the old piece of wood meant more than many of the other quaint artifacts. I cleaned it up, repaired the crack, and installed it above the new front doors in braces, much like those it used to set in at night. Near the front doors, one corner of the Store was kept in its original configuration. The three old counters—where we took weekly orders and packed groceries in boxes and paper bags and where traveling salesmen ate Vienna sausages, hoop cheese and Gibbs Pork'n Beans—were stripped of their black lacquer and refinished down to their natural golden heart pine. The rust on the old cash register was removed and it was restored to its natural gunmetal gray, then placed at its rightful home on the main counter. Twenty-five antique soft drink bottles of various brands including Pepsi, Coke, Orange Crush, and three old Mountain Dew bottles with the hillbilly running out the outhouse, were washed and placed on the original shelves behind the counter. This place had become a real neat hangout, not only for my hunting buddies, but also for my family. I can stay there for hours, examining the pictures, looking at the fire in the woodstove, or just taking in the rich hue of the counters, and reflecting back on when I was a boy, helping my mom deliver groceries and stock the canned goods. We call it "the Store."

"Daddy, can you put up my swings please?" came the request from the back seat, as we pulled up.

"Of course, Pumpkin, let me put some stuff inside and get Luke in his pen first."

"Okay, Daddy."

We took everything inside: clothing, groceries, blankie, stuffed animals, Barbie dolls, Little Debbie's—all the essentials for a weekend father/daughter getaway. "Let me vacuum first, Sarah, then we'll go outside."

"Okay, Daddy. I'll watch TV, while you do that."

I finished the vacuuming, put Luke in his pen and set up the swings on the swing set I'd built two months prior to this weekend. We played and threw the Barbie ball for about a half hour, then I told Sarah I needed to finish the fence. "Can you help Daddy?" I asked her.

"Uh huh," she replied in her drawn-out affirmation.

I began to nail boards onto the twenty four-by-four posts that I'd already placed in the ground the previous week in preparation to affix the railings this weekend. "Can you help Daddy by handing me nails whenever I need one?" I asked Sarah.

"Yes, sir!" she answered. We had finished about four posts when she exclaimed, "I'm going to swing some now, Daddy!"

"That's fine, sweetie," I said, watching her put down the nails and sprint to the swings, yelling with pure glee all the way. It did not seem like it had been almost five years since she was born and I had sat in the Daddy chair beside Susan at the hospital, holding my little girl wrapped in a blanket and hoodie—with only her face peeking out.

"Sarahface." I'd given her that first nickname because all I could see was her face. My dreams for her began then and, sometime during that first year amidst all the night feedings, diaper changes, nighttime tuck-ins, and regrets that my mother and father had not lived to see her, I'd decided to fix up the Store—another dream. I wanted her to have a connection to my family and to the farm. All three of her grandparents on my side were gone now, though she did know my stepfather, Granddaddy Alf, for a while before he passed. I wanted her to see and experience where I grew up, and here we were.

"Okay, Pumpkin." It was another nickname I'd given her. "I'm going to keep working on the fence." I hammered each nail, all the while listening to her sing her own made-up song at the top of her lungs, as she enjoyed her newfound ability to propel herself to new heights on the swing—at the exact spot where I'd played Army at her age.

"Look at me, Daddy!" she demanded, as she reached for the tallest branches of the old sycamores.

"I'm looking at you, Pump-Pump!" I shouted. This was another name for her, a contraction, abbreviation, or some derivation of Pumpkin I had devised one day while ogling over her. "You be safe now!"

"Okay, Daddy!"

In about thirty minutes, she came back to help me with the fence. After I showed her how the bubble worked in the level, she held it while I started the first nail on each railing. Sarah helped me finish three more posts, holding the level and handing me nails. Then she turned to explore the myriad oyster shells in the driveway, dumped there years ago by Alf to fill in the mud puddles.

"Daddy, what are these?" she asked, looking up at me from her squatting position, her ever-inquisitive blue eyes fully expecting the usual ultimate Daddy-answer.

"They're oyster shells. Your Granddaddy Alf dumped them there a long time ago to fill in holes. You know those oyster tongs leaning against the wall in your room? Granddaddy Alf used them to catch those oysters. Then he shucked 'em and put the shells out here."

"Can I take one home to Mommy?"

"Yes," I replied. At four, our daughter collected everything. I thought one day she might have her own museum.

"Thanks, Daddy!"

"You're welcome, Sarahface," I replied. Sarah ran back to the swing set to resume her singing, then came back later to help me with the last four posts. I was sweating and hammering away, and my back was beginning to get stiff when I heard her warn, "Don't step in those fire ants Daddy!"

"Good call, Pumpkin," I thankfully answered, as I hadn't even seen the dirt mound filled with the devilish creatures. Sarah had become familiar with them at age two when she stepped into a nice pile in our yard. After that harrowing experience, she could pick them out like a hawk zeroing in on a field mouse.

Five minutes after she told me to look out, I, of course, stepped right in them, but was able to get out quick enough to limit my bites to a mere two.

"Are you okay, Daddy? I know those bad old fire ants can hurt."

"I'm okay, darling. Thank you for asking," I answered.

"You're welcome, Daddy." As she looked up at me, her blondish hair danced in the morning sun and for a fleeting moment, her clear young eyes allowed a glimpse into the life of a four-year-old, uncluttered by the problems of the world. Her universe was her momma, who was on a trip, and her daddy, who was okay since most of those mean old fire ants didn't get him.

We finished the last post. I was tired, hungry, and thirsty, and wanted to eat lunch. "Sarah let's go and eat," I suggested.

"No!" she quickly responded. "Daddy, I want to walk down the road!"

"You mean the road right here beside the Store?" I asked.

"Yes, sir!" It was what we had always called the "rock road," since it was paved with rough asphalt made up of many rocks. Growing up, I spent many hours on that 200-yard stretch of road between Highway 304 and Granddaddy's Victorian house. The road also separated the Store from my boyhood home beside it and, as you looked directly down the road from the Store, you could see Granddaddy's house, almost framed by the end of the road itself. Someone still lives there but the yard that Grandmamma spent hours in every day to maintain its immaculate southern appearance complete with red, white, and fuchsia azaleas, blooming white dogwoods, crimson crepe myrtles, yellow daffodils, tulips of all colors, precisely trimmed hedges, and pecan trees, now bears little resemblance to that utopian yard of fifty years ago. "Yes, we can walk down the road Pumpkin." I took her hand, and we began our walk that was only a few yards for both of us, but full of adventure for her and spliced with memories for me.

"Daddy, what is that sweet smell? It smells sooooo good," Sarah asked.

"That's the honeysuckle in your Grandmamma Lois's yard." I pointed out the yellow and white entangled mass of honeysuckle vines at the edge of the yard where I grew up. The house was vacant now and had been since my stepfather passed away two years earlier. It was sold but the new owners hadn't moved in. The sweetness of the honeysuckle lingered in the air, the same as I remembered it.

"Do you remember we picked some and you sucked out the juice last year up on the farm?"

"Yes, sir. Can I have some Daddy?"

"Yes, here's some, Sarah." I picked one of the white bunches growing near the ground, customarily bit off the end and handed it to her. "Suck on that end," I instructed her.

"Uhmmm, that's good, Daddy."

"It sure is," I answered, as I tasted some from another stem. I could almost hear the leather in my catcher's mitt popping, as I played baseball in the yard with a yellow blossom in my mouth; or hear Rex, our childhood pet German Shepard, running up to lick me; or my sister yelling at me to pull the mason jar suspended on a string out of the ditch behind the house as minnows swam into it. That was our way of fishing without going to the river. The aroma hung there, suspended in the air, and in time. "Daddy, what's that old building?" Sarah asked, as we continued our walk down the rock road.

"That's our old barn." It was now dilapidated and falling down, almost to the ground, burdened by years of weather, termites and every other thing mother nature can throw at an old barn. "We used to store hay in it when I was a boy, Sarah. Before that, my Granddaddy and Great Granddaddy used it to as a shed for farm implements that were pulled by mules. Your daddy used to get up on top there with the other boys, sit on old burlap sacks and slide down that tin roof onto the flat part . . . kind of like the big slide at the beach."

"Weren't you scared, Daddy?" Sarah asked.

"I guess we never really thought about it, Pumpkin," I responded.

"My goodness!" she said, looking up at me with that little grin, shocked that her father would participate in anything the least bit risky since he was always so protective of her.

"I wouldn't let you do it, though," I confirmed.

"Daddy, tell me about that big house," she asked, as we continued our walk.

"Well Sarah, that was my grandmamma and granddaddy's house."

"Did you ever go in it?"

"Oh yes, Pumpkin, I ate dinner there every day with Grandmamma."

"You mean you ate there every night?"

"No, I ate there every day at noon," I answered.

"Oh, you mean you ate lunch," came her corrective reply.

"Yes Sarah, except we always called it dinner back then. We ate chicken and pastry, collards, dumplings, biscuits, and even rolled-up biscuits Grandmamma used to make—especially for Aunt Betty and me. We called them snake biscuits 'cause they looked like snakes to us. We had lots of butter and sugary iced tea, and the house always smelled like something good was boiling. Your great-grandmamma used to call us into the kitchen with a little bell, yelling something akin to a Bertie County hog call, where her family came from. She stretched it out and it sounded something like "Clyyyyeeeeeedddddddda," meaning Clyde, my granddaddy."

"Daddy let's walk down here," was her matter-of fact reply to my intricate reminiscing.

We turned, walked a little toward the river and passed an old yard where I used to play with the neighbors. It was so overgrown, you could barely see the old house where their ten children and I played, much less the yard.

"Sarah, we used to play football over there and that's where your daddy almost got his eye put out." Yep, I had a proverbial almost-got-my-eye-put-out story. "We were throwing reeds that we'd cut as spears. How stupid can you get? One of my friends threw one and hit me right under the eye."

"Daddy, you shouldn't have been doing that!" Sarah admonished.

"You're exactly right, Pumpkin. Don't you ever do anything like that."

"Let's walk down here," she directed, knowing she was pretty much in charge of this excursion. Even at four years old, she delighted in the obvious influence, if not control, that she had over a grown man.

We turned and headed the other way in front of the old house, toward the end of Swan Point Road. "Sarah, did you know that the original store was right in there?" I asked, as I pointed to a spot under two gargantuan sycamore trees surrounded by a maze of twenty-foot-tall shrubs.

"Where?" she peered into the trees.

"Right in there, in those bushes. You can still see the tin roof that has fallen on the ground. I remember when the old store was still standing, and we used to play in there."

"Was it fun, Daddy?"

"Oh yes, we had lots of fun. We . . ."

"Daddy!" Sarah abruptly interrupted, "Look!" She pulled me across the road to the corner of what used to be Grandmamma's yard. "Look, it's more honeysuckle!"

"I don't see any, Sarah," I replied.

"Right there, Daddy." She walked over, stooped low to the ground and sure enough, pointed out some more honeysuckle. "Daddy, can you help me?"

"Sure, Pump Pump." I bit off the end and gave it to her. As she sucked in the nectar, a growing smile filled her face. "Uhmmm, that's gooooood," she groaned.

"Sarah, are you getting hungry?" I asked.

"Yes sir."

"Why don't we go back to the Store and get some lunch?"

"Okay," she agreed. Holding hands, we headed up the rock road back toward the Store and back past the old barn, listening to the singing cardinals, multi-tune mockingbirds and chirping robins—and feeling the warm light breeze on our faces. Sarah was observing everything, her growing little mind absorbing every detail while trying to decipher all of nature's creations. She often glanced up at me.

I was looking at everything too, but mostly at her. The sun was high above the sycamore trees that encased the road, its welcome spring radiance eclipsed by the newly green leaves dancing in the wind and announcing their seasonal return by splattering their shadows down on the road. It was a supreme spring day that God had created just for us.

When we returned to the corner of my boyhood yard, Sarah said, "Daddy, let's get just one more honeysuckle from Grandmamma Lois's yard."

"Okay, Pumpkin. Let me get one for you. Here, try these." I offered her a really fragrant bunch.

She bit off the end of a yellow one like I'd shown her, put it into her mouth, sucked out the nectar, swayed back and forth, and smiled up at me with total contentment. Then she did the same thing with another white honeysuckle. This time, she gazed up at me and announced, "You know what, Daddy, the yellow ones are the sweetest. I like them the best."

"You know what, Sarah, I think you're right. I do too," I replied.

She grinned up at me, and I grinned back.

As I stood there, all the unnecessary insignificant mess that had been stored in mind over the last forty years—since I'd first tasted those same honeysuckle—now melted away, replaced by the simple innocence on my daughter's face. It was one of those fleeting moments God gives you as a daddy, as a person, like a brief shooting star in a winter sky. At that instant, you know what is truly important in this world. You want more of these moments, but you know you're eternally blessed with the ones you get.

"Daddy, let's eat," she pronounced, as she turned toward the Store.

Arriving back at the Store, we scooted up to one of the counters I'd refinished, where many salesmen in the forties, fifties, and sixties, had eaten their lunches off our fancy plates of wax paper. That day, Sarah ate her peanut butter and jelly "swamiche," as she called it, and Goldfish off a paper plate. I ate my usual ham sandwich. We looked at each other across the counter, winking and smiling. I playfully stole some of her Goldfish, as she giggled.

After lunch, we again went outside. I started framing up the new woodshed, while she played on the swing set. Later, she helped me by handing me nails and the level, as I once again tried to use some of my eighth-grade shop skills.

Around 3:00 p.m., we both got tired and headed inside to watch cartoons. She snuggled close to me, and I draped my arm around her, holding her tight as I napped. It's hard to explain the feeling you get while hugging your four-year-old little girl close on the couch with her head resting on your chest. You know she's safe with you, the outside world held at bay. And no matter what the future holds, she looks to you during those special years for all answers. And to you, she is the answer. None of my naps were ever as content as those spent holding her—before or since. As evening approached, we rode up to the Burger King where Sarah got a kid's meal with chicken tenders, and I got a chicken sandwich. We sat side by side in the booth; she played with her toy, leaned over and hugged me. She told me she loved me. I ate my sandwich with one hand and held her tight with my other arm. It was not a five-star restaurant, but I would not have traded it for anything in Manhattan.

"Sarah, do you want some ice cream?" I asked, having less doubt about her answer than the inevitability of death and taxes.

"Yeah!!!!!" came the reply. "Daddy, is there a Baskin-Robbins in the County?"

"No Pumpkin, but I've got a plan," I assured her.

"Okay, Daddy, I'm ready to go."

We left Burger King, headed down the road, pulled into a convenience store, got two Eskimo bars and some bread for Sunday, and went back out to the car to eat the two ice cream bars—right there in the parking lot.

"Sarah, did you get any in your mouth?" I asked, as I spied the chocolate-stained face of my once-clean daughter in the rearview mirror. I could barely see her teeth and half of a nose through the smeared chocolate.

"Uh huh," she responded, grinning, and spreading the chocolate out so she looked like a dark brown Cheshire cat.

"Let's go ride around the field," I suggested, as I cleaned her up with a wet wipe.

"Okay, Daddy."

We had driven Sarah around the farm fields since she was born. She'd already seen numerous turkeys, deer, bear, and even a coyote and a bobcat. We turned up the Alfred Swamp Road and I blurted, "Sarah, look over there. There are some turkeys!"

"Wow Daddy, how many is there?"

"One, two . . . five, Sarah!"

"Yeah, Daddy! What is that?" Sarah asked, looking out the passenger window.

"It looks like a fire," I replied, examining the large plume of smoke billowing to the northeast.

"Let's go find it!" she immediately countered.

"But Sarah, I don't know if we'll be able to find it."

"Daddy I really want to find it!"

"Well, let's finish riding the fields, and then we'll find the fire, okay?"

We rode around the fields for another twenty minutes, but Sarah kept asking about the fire, so we ended up driving to Mesic.

From there, I could tell the fire was near Hobucken, a few more miles away. But my daughter was getting sleepy, so I came up with a choice. "Sarah, you're getting sleepy. We can go see the fire or go back to the Store. Which one do you want to do?"

"I want to go see the fire!" was her confident response.

We drove toward Hobucken, and as we rounded a corner in the highway and came up on the small bridge at the head of Jones Bay, something was in the middle of the highway. I slowed down. "Sarah, look at that bobcat!" I shouted.

"Wow, Daddy!"

The bobcat was stalking something on the shoulder of the road and didn't want to move. But when we got within ten yards of him, he leapt into the marsh.

"Sarah, that's your second bobcat! Do you know how old Daddy was before I saw two bobcats?"

"Ninety-nine years old, Daddy?"

"No, I was thirty," I assured her, shaking my head and laughing.

"Daddy, that's oooooooold!" she declared.

"I know, Pumpkin. Daddy's getting on up there. Sarah, look at that smoke. I think it's around the north side of Jones Bay somewhere."

"Let's go, Daddy!"

We rode all the way down to the end of the paved road and stopped on a bridge where years before I had gone deer hunting with my Granddaddy.

"There it is Sarah, at the mouth of Drum Creek. Do you see it?"

"Yeah, I see it, Daddy! Is it going to get us?"

"No Sarah, we're safe."

"Okay, Daddy."

"Are you ready to go now?" I asked.

"Yes, sir. Thank you for taking me to see the fire, Daddy."

"You're welcome, Pumpkin," I responded, glancing in the rearview mirror at my sleepy but content child. She looked back at me, her eyelids blinking heavily.

We drove back over the high-rise bridge and came to where we'd seen the bobcat just a few minutes before.

"He's gone, Pumpkin," I observed, as I turned in the seat.

My little girl was slumped in her car seat with her head turned to the side, sleeping. She'd seen her fire and she was happy.

When we got back to the Store, I carried her in and laid her down to get her undressed and ready for bed. She woke up and I gave her a bath, as she played with her mermaid and puffer fish. I expect at that time, we had the only hunting camp in the County with a mermaid and puffer fish in the shower—but my buddies did not mind.

After I dried her hair and she put on her princess nightgown, Sarah curled up in my lap and we rocked in the glider while listening to the same nighttime melodies we'd played for her since she was born. She felt soft and warm and, as I held her, I knew that moment would never be long enough. The low music filled the same room where I used to run and play; where Mom used to watch me through the window as I maneuvered toy Army men in the dirt below. Sarah grew heavy and limp in my arms signaling another bedtime was near. Rising from the glider, I gently laid her in bed and pulled the covers up to her Sarahface.

I kissed her goodnight and whispered, "Daddy loves you." She couldn't hear my words, but I could—and Mom could. Pausing at the door, I stopped as usual and gazed at her; she was my life, and I did not want that day to end.

Relaxing in my recliner, I pulled out an old 1974 *Sports Afield* from the bookcase. Daylight was fading, the window was open in my bedroom and the TV was off. I fidgeted with some pages but finally put down the magazine. I kept thinking about the day and how we'd shared some of the same things I'd experienced when I was a boy.

As dusk neared, the whippoorwills started up behind the Store, the last cardinals tweeted—signaling to all the last remaining breaths of light—and the honeysuckle sweetened the air. It had been a right good day.

The next morning, we got up and ate muffins and cereal for

breakfast, then shot the BB gun out behind the store. I held Sarah in front of me, helping her look down the barrel as she tried to hit a pie plate placed at the base of one of the sycamores. She hit it several times and got excited each time, jumping up to check the target, then running back to me for a congratulatory hug.

Later in the morning, we drove to the farm and threw the dummies for Luke to retrieve, watching him jump high and then splash enthusiastically into the water. After each retrieve, Sarah turned to me and giggled and then gave Luke a big hug—just like I'd given her when she shot the BB gun.

After an hour or so, we returned to the Store and started packing up for the ride home.

"Daddy, I want to give this oyster shell to Momma," she said, holding a prize from yesterday's foray in the driveway.

"Okay," I said.

We loaded everything up into the Suburban, including Luke; we locked the Store and got ready to head out. Before we drove off, I turned to look at Sarah. There she was, all strapped into her car seat, wearing blue jeans, a pink t-shirt, and a ball cap, almost five years old and grinning at her daddy. Again, it seemed like just yesterday that Susan and I had taken her home from the hospital—two days old, wrapped up in a blanket. A close friend had told me then that the feeling we had when Sarah was born would just keep getting better. I didn't think that could be possible, but it was; it had gotten even better.

"I had a good time with you at the Store, Sarah," I told her, as I patted her knee.

"I did too, Daddy. Thanks for taking me to the Store. When will Momma be home?"

Tying Nets

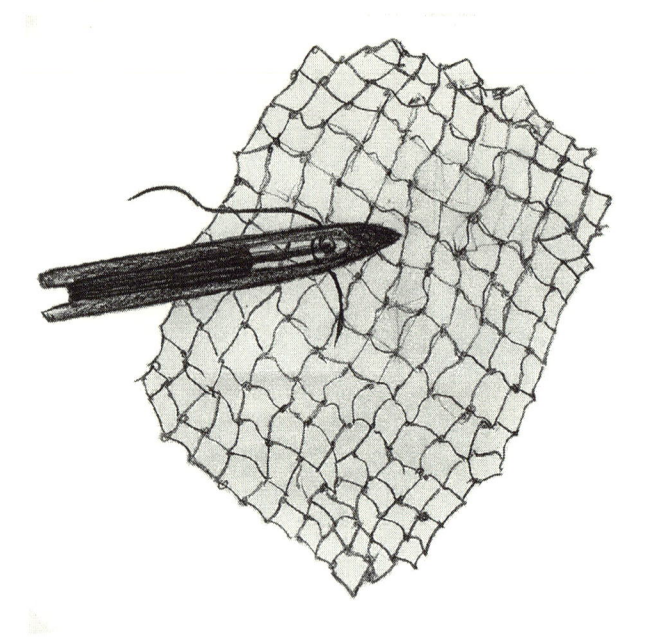

There are many things I wish I could to do before I leave this earth: learn to play the acoustic guitar, stalk an Alaskan moose with a bow, return to Saskatchewan and spend fading afternoons scouting ducks and chilly fresh September mornings shooting them on my own without a guide. I'd like to walk our farm one more day with a favorite bird dog and find that sunset covey, apologize to certain people for not handling a few things the right way, visit Normandy, and understand how the rural men of my youth mended nets.

TYING NETS

In the '60s, when I played Little League, wore Opie dungarees and white Chuck Taylors and watched Motor Mouse and Johnny Quest, we would regularly ride to Hobucken to go fishing at the draw bridge. Invariably, on the way down, I'd gaze at sun-leathered men in t-shirts toiling in their yards. Hunched over a gill net, shrimp net, or crab net stretched between two pine trees in the yard, they deftly maneuvered long pieces of pointed wood, magically joining together strands of cotton or mono, and getting their rigs ready to work again for their families. How they were able to "sew" a net always fascinated me. Shoot, in those years I'd just learned to tie a cinch knot on my double-hook red-bead rigs, taught to me by a stranger who fished for kings at the end of Sportsman's Pier at Atlantic Beach. Seeing the local men tend to these nets in their yards, amid the smoking tar vats that were used to soak them after reparations were done, was just as common back then as the small trawlers these men piloted back and forth across Bay River. This type of fishing has all but disappeared now, a victim of economics, politics, and what is typically called progress. But like my physics professor used to say, each action has an equal and opposite reaction, and with the decline of traditional subsistence fishing, so has come the advent of more and more sport boats, trout poppers, redfish rigs, non-honor system boat ramps, and the dollars and influxes they all bring. I can usually tell where someone was raised, or better yet not raised, or their real affinity to eastern North Carolina, simply by their response to one question about one fish. So help me, right up there with reciting our state motto, I believe it ought to be a requirement that in order to live in North Carolina, at least east of Raleigh, you must answer this one question correctly: Now Fisherperson, what is this fish called?

Fisherperson Number 1: "Oh yes, that's a redfish right there. I cast flies for those bad boys off the new tower on my new light blue flats rig, while wearing my pastel casting pants and shirt."

ANNNKKKK! Wrong Eleanor!

Fisherperson Number 2: "That's a drum, bud. Lil' puppy . . . bunch of 'em use in the fall off Maw Point."

Ding Ding Ding! We have a winner! Come on over tonight pard. Let's have some fried croakers, collards, and dumplings—and I don't mean pastry. Oh, I'm sure my suggestion for citizenry qualification likely won't happen, as it's more likely than a Lowland flood on a three-day northeast blow that the N. C. Department of Commerce would have a Piedmont cow at just the suggestion. Don't get me wrong: I'm an avid sport fisherman, always have been. I like nothing better than to catch rock (not striped bass) with a buck tail at Mann's Harbor, or with a fluke on the Roanoke. Most of my life, including now, there have been few things I would rather do than cast, cast, and cast again, trying to lure that bass out of the lily pads or speck off the grass at high tide.

As a boy, I fished almost every day during the long summers with my faithful Mitchell 300. But when I was young and my stepdad asked me to go "netting" with him, I always looked forward to it. It was different. It was my connection to the grounded, knowing men in their yards and to our area's history. And somehow, I knew I needed to know more than I pretended I thought I did.

It was a very hot day in July of 1974 when Alf popped his head in the den and asked if I wanted to go netting with him and Mr. Rudolph. I'd already been down to the river that day and had only caught a measly two croakers. *All My Children* just wasn't getting it done, so I was eager to see what we could do with the net.

"Sure," I responded.

We hooked up the boat, checked the gas and headed out to pick up Mr. Rudolph. Alf and Mr. Rudolph had grown up together in Mesic, worked together for the Corps of Engineers on the Hobucken draw bridge, and often fished together. Mr. Rudolph didn't hunt like most of us back then, but he sure did like to gill net. And he also liked to garden. He and Alf shared a garden that was probably an acre in size. When it came time to dig potatoes, and all of us kids had to pitch in, it seemed like that fairly adequate one-acre plot was bigger than any of the giant corn fields in Pamlico County.

The largest and most burdensome that piece of salt-intruded border-line marsh ever seemed was the last time I ever dug potatoes, just after my high school graduation night. The mosquitoes were eating me up; I was filthy and sweaty, and it must have been at least 125 degrees. I swear I think it's against the law to dig potatoes without mosquitoes buzzing in your ear, sweaty mud getting in your eyes and covering your scratched to-a-pulp mosquito bites, and the sun beating down on your back making sure it all mixes with the three gallons of repellant to form a concoction just short of rat poison in toxicity. Just delightful. Yes sir, bud. I swore to myself then, at what I thought was the all-knowing age of eighteen, that I'd never have a garden, and certainly never dig potatoes—nope, not this guy, not ever.

Well, I have since had a garden, enjoy it immensely, and savor every squash and string bean that comes out of it. But ain't no potatoes grown in it.

I slipped over to the middle of the sticky bench seat in Alf's '68 Chevy pickup, my legs sticking to the vinyl like an egg without PAM. Mr. Rudolph got in and he and Alf exchanged the usual greeting, which consisted of a kind of mutual grunt that was common among men in their fifties, in the 1970s, in the country where I grew up. I think if one of them had actually managed to utter some jovial demonstrative, "Hello!"-type greeting, I would have grown an inch more hair right there, probably irritating my balding stepfather even more.

Back then, I always wondered why they didn't speak more, like we boys did when we got together and played ball or rode Honda 70s. Of course, now in my own sixties, I see the wise virtues of less conversation, the balanced efficiency of knowing what a long-time friend is thinking, and the confident smartness of knowing that he knows what you're thinking. *Why waste time talking about it? Got it now.*

Because you could leave from there and be at several stops within ten minutes, we headed to Bear Creek to put in, a fairly large deep-water creek just off the mouth of Bay River. Alf backed the old boat into the creek until the Evinrude was covered good and Mr. Rudolph and I teamed up to push it off the trailer. Our boat was a nondescript center-console nineteen-foot fiberglass working boat. It wasn't meant for poling the flats in pursuit of redfish, nor gliding around silently via an electric motor looking for large mouths—or "chubs," as some of the older men called them. It was meant to put meat on the table in any way possible. In addition to the ever-present gill net on the bow, it had also been outfitted with eyebolts on the transom to which we could affix our shrimp trawl when the creeks opened in July.

In the early '70s, at the opening of shrimp season, a man who knew what he was doing—and Alf did—could take a small rig up Bear Creek and Little Bear Creek to corral the newly matured crustaceans as they headed out of the nurseries. We spent several opening July mornings drifting at the mouths of those creeks, waiting patiently for the season to open. Slowly rolling there in the predawn steamy haze, bathed in the approaching eastern orangeness and gazing toward the easter'd flashing channel markers bouncing their greens and reds off the water's sheen, we'd sit—an experienced waterman and a young teenager, edging toward go time. Only the constant hummings of larger boats in the Sound was louder than the ticking of our watches that we both checked every five minutes, like daddies pacing for after-midnight teenage daughters returning late from their dates with knuckleheads. We were more than ready to pitch doors into the murky depths of the creek, eagerly guessing what could be dumped on the cull board in an hour or so.

I can remember one standout summer day, around my twelfth year, heading back to the ramp with 400 pounds of shrimp. Our gunwales were so close to the water we looked like a center console kayak. Mom went to Sears that day and bought a freezer. We ate those shrimp for two years. Like the old movie line, we had fried shrimp, boiled shrimp, shrimp salad, shrimp sandwiches—but we had no shrimp scampi. I didn't even know what that was until I was thirty.

But today was for netting fish and, as we readied the boat, securing the canvas tarp over the net, we set our gaze toward the mouth of Bear Creek. Alf parked the truck, while Mr. Rudolph and I loaded the boat with coolers. After Alf started her up and idled the required warm up time to make sure she was running okay, I hopped in, pushing off the dock with my feet. We motored out toward the mouth of the creek to a little side cove and stopped there "to get our mess right," as I still say today to the amusement of my daughter, who also uses it now when she turkey hunts with me.

"Let me get my mess right, Daddy," she says, as I'm trying to get her hustled out the door so we can hear the first owl hoots. Kids are like regurgitating sponges. I reckon pretty soon she'll be telling me I've "mommicked" something up.

The seagulls were squawking high above us, the trawlers mulled about searching the river for its afternoon gifts, and all around us the semi-salt aroma enveloped the stagnant air and usual gray summer haze.

"Let's head over to Spring Creek," came Mr. Rudolph's suggestion.

Alf agreed, turning her to the southeast, across Bay River, toward Bonners Bay. Approaching the mouth of the creek, we slowly eased up to one of the points of marsh. As always, I was at the bow since it was my job to throw the weights just off the bank. We didn't have anchors or any other store-bought weights to keep the net from drifting, so we used whatever was handy. Actually, it wasn't until a few years ago when I was tearing some juniper siding off an old farm cabin that I realized what our net weights actually were. As I stripped some of the siding away, I saw a cylindrical metal object hanging in the space beside the window. It was a counterweight used to raise and lower the windows. *So that's what we used forty years ago,* I thought. Funny how memories return given the slightest provocation, having been secured in a vault locked by insignificant stuff for so long. The torpedo-shaped weights were perfect for throwing and did the job, as long as there was minimal wind.

Once I had the weight out, Alf reversed the boat and the meticulously folded net rolled off the bow, as we headed to the far point. My job was to ensure it didn't get hung up.

Once we reached the other side of the mouth, I threw the weight into the water, again trying to get it as close to the bank as possible. If I messed up, I usually heard about it via a familiar frustrated sigh, no doubt wondering why it was so hard for a not-paying-attention fourteen-year-old boy to land a weight near the bank. In turn, I wished I didn't have to hear a retort if I missed the bank... but knowing full-well I should have been paying more attention. Back then, that was how you learned to do right.

Mr. Rudolph was always quiet, sometimes interjecting a suggestion for me. With the net out, we motored up to the head of the creek. From there, Alf steered the boat slowly back and forth from creek side to creek side, while Mr. Rudolph and I rhythmically slammed the water with long poles that had been cut and shaved from local trees.

As we crisscrossed the creek, our hope was to drive the fish into the net; it was sort of like hounds to the hunters. I've since seen this technique used on TV by native fishermen in some remote Amazon areas. And I had the unmitigated temerity to think this idea was unique to Mesic?

Once we decided we had sufficiently scared a bunch of fish to the mouth, we pulled up to one side of the net, bow facing into the wind. Alf and Mr. Rudolph began pulling in the net, tossing fish in the tub behind them. Though different from fishing with my rod and reel, it was always exciting to see what got caught in the net. Usually puppy drum, croakers, trout, and flounder were the mainstays. Sometimes, we'd catch jumping mullet or even turtles. The turtles never got hurt and were always released. But every once in a while, we'd keep a mess of the jumpers, and then have a mullet roast in the yard. This ceremonial roast consisted of putting a fifteen-foot roll of tin foil down in the yard, and then dumping charcoal on it and lighting it. Once the fire got hot, we'd impale the butterflied paprika and pepper-laden mullets onto metal stakes, scales still on, and lean them over the coals, meat to the flame. It would take about thirty minutes for them to cook, while the oil dripped down the stakes onto the coals and yard the whole time. The local service station didn't produce that much used grease during $6 oil change Mondays.

After sufficient time, the mullets were removed from the stakes and plopped onto paper plates with slaw, hush puppies, potato salad, string beans or whatever anyone brought. You had to wolf it down fast because if the mullet sat for any length of time, it would get right strong and the prissiest of the bunch wouldn't eat it. Among the flurry of activity, everyone got a plate filled with all the accompaniments and then the chomping, talking, laughing, and catching up would continue. The men would attend to the stakes, getting more fish for whomever needed any, always admonishing us kids to stay away from coals. The ladies would help serve the fixings, usually in a slightly more compassionate tone.

I don't remember anybody actually eating all the fish on their plate like you might consume nice flounder, but it was really the experience we all craved—socializing for the adults and novelty excitement for the kids. For me, it was also a connection to the idolized past existence of my relatives, brought to life out of a picture we had of Granddaddy and (Great) Uncle Ralph on the banks of the Inland Waterway—sometime in the 1950s, mullets just-a-smoking.

That night, every cat from the neighborhood would come to visit and, if we shined a flashlight into the yard, it would look like the African Serengeti, complete with leopard-like growls and maybe a brave anteater-like possum. These mullet roasts were some of my most treasured memories growing up and I still have Alf's homemade metal stakes, placed neatly on a shelf at the store. It was a lot of trouble to put on a roast, and we didn't do it a lot, but like many things that really matter in life, it was your perception of the experience that counted, not necessarily the efficacy of what we were actually doing. I'm sure some of the snobbish TV cooks nowadays wouldn't even entertain eating a lowly mullet, let alone want to clean up the mess afterwards. But tofu on a bed of lettuce with a raspberry sauce doesn't even come close to mullets in August, the smell of smoldering charcoal, hush puppies frying, fresh-cut tomatoes, and the sound of a six-and-a-half-ounce bottle of Coke being popped open with the bottle opener hanging by a string on the side of the table, and then the taste of that ice cold drink—no, not "soda"—going down. To this day, I drink Coke from a can only begrudgingly.

After dinner, the yard was cleaned up, oily tin foil put in the garbage and the stakes cleaned in a bucket with Joy, then left out to dry. Last, I would dump the scraps in the ditch behind the house— no doubt sealing their fate as possum fodder for the evening. The only evidence of the feast would be the oblong burnt patch of grass in our yard that stayed that way for a few weeks, finally replaced by the kudzu-like centipede. For some reason, I always thought it was kind of cool to have that patch in our yard. My city neighbors now would probably be horrified, but they've seen everything from ducks to turkeys taken from my truck into our garage, so maybe a piece of burnt grass in our in-town yard would not faze them. "Lost cause," they'd say, "that County boy."

Just before I got out of college, when Mom went to Canada with my aunts and uncles, Alf and I were batching it. He asked me what I wanted for dinner, and I suggested he and I have a mullet roast. It had been fifteen years since we'd put one on, and I could see the twinkle in his eye. He and I ate good that night. Later, we listened to the cats, or "sons of bitches," as he called them, growl at each other near the dying coals. I drank from a can of Coke that night, but we washed the stakes in Joy.

...

Slowly and methodically, Alf and Mr. Rudolph pulled in the net, one section at a time, pausing to discard sticks or cans or whatever trash was caught, shaking the net like a bed sheet at spring cleaning and resuming only after each section was neatly re-deposited onto the bow. Every fish was slipped through the monofilament mesh, examined, and then thrown in the tub behind them or pitched back—seed to grow another day.

My job was to keep the boat idling, speed-up if needed, and keep it positioned so we remained at a 180-degree angle to the net, all-the-while keeping an anxious eye on the catch coming over the bow. The number of fish that were lurking in these creeks that I evidently could not catch with a rod and reel always amazed me. Each croaker, trout, or puppy flapping over that bow not only propped up my hopes when I got back to my Mitchell, it also gave me more patience to always keep fishing, to make that last cast, thinking a bite was just around the corner. I began to realize—after seeing them stuck in the nets—that the fish were definitely there; you just had to catch them. To this day, I hate to pack it in at the end of any fishing day, always envisioning a lunker at the end of the next cast, or last cast, or next-to-the last cast. After the net and end weights were pulled in, the canvas was folded over it. Then, all the fish and any crabs were separated into assigned Coleman metal coolers, and we paused to get our mess right, while deciding where to go next.

That day, it wasn't Little Bear or another creek off Bonners Bay; it was Shaddocks' Creek. So off we sped to Shaddocks' and back across Bay River.

I liked Shaddocks' Creek. It was where Alf first took me duck hunting at age nine. My feet were cold, and we didn't see any ducks until late in the afternoon. But just when we were getting ready to leave, a flock of canvasbacks zoomed in—breast up—and our guest, Mr. Lloyd, knocked out two. The long elegantly necked divers were much bigger than the sparrows I was used to shooting with my Daisy. As I rubbed the soft black-cherry feathers on their heads and admired them, utterly awed that such a wild and beautiful creature could exist, I was hooked right there at the ripe age of nine on this life's adventure of hunting and fishing. From that day on, I loved being in nature—despite any cold feet. As it turned out that summer day, we didn't catch many at Shaddocks'. We did, however, manage to get a cooler full at the other usual locations later on. At each creek, we reenacted the whole process, motoring up to the bank, throwing the weight, backing the net off the bow, slamming the poles and picking up the net. It was workmanlike and perhaps not deserving of a glowing representation on some of the glitzy TV sports shows of the times that had as guests marlin fishermen wearing captain's hats, but it was how it was done back then. It put fish on the table in a hurry. Yet, it still soothed our outdoor souls with a smidgeon of sportiness, allowing us to touch nature up close, rewarding us for a yeoman's job of hard work. It embellished us with the saltiness of the marshes, the laughter of the gulls, the swaying of the pines on the banks of Jones Island, and the occasional curious co-captaining of dolphins bouncing alongside our bow.

In those brief afternoons, we were partners, participants, and partakers in the bounties of the estuarine tributaries of eastern North Carolina, what present-day self-proclaimed environmentalists call one of Earth's rare ecosystems. We just called it home. The rushes and creeks were pure and genuine, and gill netting back then was as much a part of the locality as corn on dark land, quail in the hedgerows, and oysters in December. Back at the dock, we secured the boat, split the trout, croakers, and crabs in the coolers with Mr. Rudolph, then dropped him off at his house.

"Goodbye Mr. Rudolph." I waved out the window.

Without looking, Alf uttered, "We'll see ya."

"Awwlright," came the over-the-shoulder reply, as Mr. Rudolph carried off his fish.

When we got home, Alf and I gathered around the cleaning table and being well-trained, I started scaling and cutting off heads while beating off the neighborhood cats with an occasional leg thrust. Still, I took selfish pride in choosing which lucky tom got the throwaway bounty. Alf did the filleting, skillfully gliding the keen knife down the backbone, flipping the fish over and doing it again, then tossing the skeleton to the cats. Alf always grouched that he hated cats, but he made sure they each got a piece and he chased off the hoggish ones.

That night, Mom dressed the fillets with corn meal and fried them up in the skillet. We also had string beans, slaw, cornbread and French-fries cut from our own potatoes—grown in that dang garden. Afterwards, Mom lit candles, trying to get what she called "that fishy smell out of the house." Neither Alf nor I ever worried about it much. I fashioned it as the smell of victory, a quick and rare but efficient conquest of the quarry I too often unsuccessfully sought with my Mitchell.

If I'd smoked or drank at fourteen, it would have been time for a cigar or brown liquor drink. I was content then, as I am now, with a Little Debbie.

In my hustling life today, I don't get to eat mullet or even croakers as much as I'd like. I haven't hunted moose yet, but don't count me out on that. I probably won't learn to play the acoustic guitar. Normandy is still on the docket. I may never chase another sundown covey on the farm again. But I have slammed an ash pole into the surface of Spring Creek and watched too aging friends with rough-tanned arms and wisdom pull in a gill net, stoically relaying their expertise of a bygone era. Like Granddaddy, I've eaten mullet over charcoal and, even though I don't go there much, I know where the drum are off Maw Point. And I can tell a croaker from a trout at the end of the line, before I hear him croaking.

Unfortunately, I never see men in the old yards mending nets anymore. A new generation of duck hunters have bought much of the land near home, setting up blinds in some of the same marshes we fished and hunted. Most of the local men that do still fish probably just buy new nets anyway, perhaps converts into our disposable lifestyles. Regardless, I would still like to learn how they used to do it. It may not be up there with the mysteries of the pyramids, but to me it's important. It's a tie—not just in the nets—but to my childhood. Maybe I'll look it up on the internet. No, I'll find someone out there who still knows. Maybe they can teach me how to plant potatoes, too? ·

Taking Her Place

My father was not a trapper, nor my grandfathers, nor my stepfather. In fact, I wasn't a trapper until just a few years ago when beavers began backing up water on the farm and the only trappers I knew really didn't want to bother with them unless they could justify it by trapping coyotes or foxes. So out of necessity and with a good dash of, "Shoot, I can do that," I bought some conibears and a few leg-holds and set up some traps in runways and channels, fully expecting to catch a decoy sled full of the fat rodents during the first night.

I caught one little beaver over the next three weeks, as he came out of the lodge into a half-drained duck impoundment. It took me a full and humbling two years to catch the momma, a forty-five-pounder, with a snare. The riser in the impoundment began flowing again and her blanket in the shape of a hat now sits on my gun rack. Right then, the trapping bug hit me hard and, at fifty-one, I was done—hooked, infatuated, and smitten like a sixth-grade boy. I'd spent my whole life outdoors, hunting squirrels first, then doves, quail, ducks, deer, and turkey and, of course, fishing for croakers and trout in the river behind our house. Trapping wasn't even thought about until I walked around a farm one day with a trapper who had caught some bobcats, foxes and coyotes.

"I could get into this trapping thing, if I ever tried it," I mentioned to my wife that evening.

New projects were always on my horizon and the last one, renovating our family's old country store and turning it into a hunting camp, had just been completed. The old store was where I'd spent many days as a boy with my mother packing groceries for neighborhood customers. With its many photos, heart of pine counters and all kinds of hunting and family memorabilia; it's a palpable connection to my childhood and to my father who passed away from cancer when I was two years old. I supposed trapping could be the new project since it also seemed to be a natural expansion of my love of hunting, conservation, and nature. My goal was to use it to manage the predator populations on the farm. The reading began and the gathering of all information was relentless. I bought some Duke leg-holds and thought if I could trap that huge beaver after two persevering years, surely catching turkey-eating coyotes and quail-killing bobcats would be at least possible. I studied, read several books, and sat in front of the computer before supper, annoying Susan with the barrage of internet instructors and reveling in her look of, "They actually have that stuff on the internet?"

Some fur was caught, and some missed, but my goal to learn and continue to improve was being achieved. No other outdoor pastime forces you to pay more attention to details, learn more about an animal's practices and habits, and frankly makes you a better woodsman and outdoorsman than trapping. In order to force an animal to place its foot in a four-inch diameter space within a thousand varied acres, you must study it and be aware of its instincts, strengths, weaknesses and what drives it at different times of the year. It's been enjoyable and now I'm catching a few coyotes, cats and coons, though not as much as I would like because I have a full-time job and live twenty miles away from our farm.

Starting in my fifties, I had a new desire to improve the quality of the outdoor experience, whether it be bow hunting more versus gun hunting, or planting and preparing duck ponds and dove fields, and watching others enjoy shooting woodies and teal in the impoundments or doves over sunflowers.

I absolutely relish the careful scouting required in November to prepare for the opening day of trapping season. Of course, the most rewarding times have been those spent with Sarah, watching her grow and learn about animals and nature. If you have children and grew up in the outdoors, you know what I mean. When the chill hits the air in October, you still get excited—but there grows a desire to pass it on to someone and watch your childhood reborn in the next generation.

From the time Sarah was a few days old, Susan and I had her out on the farm. She's grown up running with Luke, walking through the hardwood swamps, squirrel hunting or coloring under the white oaks, turkey hunting on spring mornings and dove hunting over sunflowers with our close friends. So even though her passion is performing on stage in plays and singing, a gift that still mystifies my wife and me, she also enjoys rambling around the countryside with her daddy, driving the Mule, learning about the outdoors and listening to my stories about the "olden days" of the seventies, eighties, and nineties.

One particular February, during her pre-teen years, I had the whole last week of trapping season off and Sarah was out of school. We planned to stay at the store, check traps, shoot the .22, squirrel hunt and sit by the fire pit. Of course, that would need to be interspersed with the *Wizards of Waverly Place, Dog with a Blog* and *Good Luck Charlie* re-runs, but that was okay. It was a deal, especially considering I could spend the entire week with her on my turf, further instilling in her a respect for the land and its wildlife and giving her the knowledge of nature that will always be with her. This is something I vowed to do from the moment I looked into her blue eyes when she was born. The first day, after we shot the .22, I set up two conibears for coons and four coyote/bobcat leg hold traps. The coon traps were baited with sardines and the canine/cat sets were dirt holes, containing deer scraps from the fall harvest with coyote and cat urine sprinkled on the backing. I'd caught three coyotes just a week earlier and was excited about the possibility of further hurting the fawn-eater population.

That night in the old store, surrounded by the warmth from the woodstove pinging with popping coals of split oak and maple, I read old issues of *Fur, Fish and Game,* and then slowly gazed through pages of the photo albums, monuments to thirty years of my hunting past. Susan sat in her self-claimed "Queen's" recliner inches from the woodstove, reading her book, and Sarah watched the Disney Channel. Looking up from the photo albums, surveying the counters and store shelves, I was humbled by the eighty-plus years of pictures—black and white, color, faded, amber portraits of good times: full duck straps, my grandfather in brown canvas hunting clothes, my stepfather with friends at the creek holding up blackheads, deer on the front of Model As with family gathered around, Mom with setters and pointers in our back yard, and a picture of me as a young man with my setter and pointer in a russet November bean field right beside a picture of my father with a pointer jumping up on his chest—all glimmering in the fire light—and shimmering even more in my memories. That's what it's all about when you're my age: family traditions, cured in the fall woods and served up to a new generation, eager to partake. But you must build that appetite. Indeed, it may never develop. Yet, if you don't prepare the meal, the appetite will undoubtedly subside, fed instead by a constant barrage of those abhorrent electronic pastimes. I've tried my best to give this appetite to my daughter or vowed to at least go down swinging. If she can one day find in nature just one-tenth of the peace I have felt in the woods and fields, she'll be forever changed, and stronger because of it.

The next morning broke cold and clear. A pinkish hue was stretching over Bay River to the east as I drove the Mule down the farm road, the cold air hitting me in the face and deflected only by the excitement of the anticipated catch. As I neared the impoundment, I made a turn in front of the first set, saw nothing, then continued toward the second set. Halfway down the dike, something sprung up in the air near my trap and kept jumping for a few seconds before hunkering down. I stopped the Mule and walked toward the bobcat, a beautiful female, snarling and hissing and growling in the trap; she was much more vocal than other cats I'd caught.

Quickly, I jumped back in the Mule and headed toward the store. After telling my wife about the cat, I hurried into Sarah's room, leaned over, and whispered, "Pumpkin, Daddy has something in the trap, if you want to come."

She slowly turned, sleepy-eyed "Is it a coyote?" she asked, as she sat upright.

"I'm not going to tell you, but if you want to come, then we need to go."

She awoke all the way up and got out of bed; then the normal ritual of an eleven-year-old girl getting dressed commenced.

After all clothes were gathered, we hopped in the Mule and waved goodbye to my wife. Susan always supported my desire to indoctrinate Sarah to these experiences, knowing how much it meant to me and recognizing the benefits it could have for our daughter. I hugged Sarah close for the cold ride, me with my beaver hat and her with her orange toboggan and camo jacket, hustling down the same road where my father undoubtedly hurried toward a morning covey sixty years ago.

As we rolled up to the place where I'd parked before, the barrage started.

"What is it, Daddy?" came her excited questions. "What did you get?"

"I'm not going to tell you," I said, holding back.

"Daddy, is it a coyote?"

"I'm not going to tell you. You'll have to see. Here's your .22. What's the first thing you do?"

"Check to see if it's loaded."

"Okay, baby girl, let's roll."

She followed me down the dike. "Daddy, will it get loose?"

"No, Pumpkin, its fine." Just then, the cat bounced up.

"Daddy, it's a bobcat!" she wailed. She walked confidently up to the cat until she got about ten yards from it. It was growling and staring at her.

"Daddy?"

"Don't worry, Sarah, you'll be fine," I reassured her.

As she walked around the cat for a picture, it slowly turned its head toward her, snarling and hissing. It then turned again to look at me.

"Wow Daddy, he's beautiful."

"Yes, she is. Sarah . . . but she'll also take some of the quail on the farm or ducks around the edge of the impoundment, so we're helping save some of those baby birds." I could see the fascination in her eyes, as they stayed riveted on this wild creature; a secretive, allusive animal that most people never see in the wild. Yet, this was the sixth bobcat Sarah had seen in the wild. I, myself, had not seen any by her age. There are no video games or TV shows that can match this type of excitement, nor make such impressions on her mind as she was taking in right there—the glistening winter grass with the morning mist rising, the brown earth of the farm fields next to the dike; the faint scent of the .22 powder after I dispatched the cat, and the clang of the trap chain as I remade the set, all combined to make this one of those times all of us live to remember. We put the bobcat and a possum, also taken right next to the cat, in the back of the Mule and headed toward the hardwoods. Sarah was excited now.

"What else do we have, Daddy?"

"I don't know, Pump-Pump, I didn't check the coon traps. Let's see!"

We walked through the same woods, where I shot my first squirrel at twelve, past the same beech trees and white oaks where she and I had waited for squirrels and colored Barbie books when she was five, to where the traps were set. A big fat boar coon was caught in one of them. "Sarah, look," I said.

"Daddy, we got one!"

"We sure did."

She watched, as I re-sprung the conibear and got the coon out, a nice one by N.C. standards. I handed it to her, and she held it up with both hands.

"Wow, he's heavy! And he is sooooo soft."

I reset the trap, freshened it with sardines and got the camera out for a picture. "Get next to the bear tree," I directed. We have several of these territorial pine marker trees where the bears scratch and chew every year. One of our traditions is taking pictures beside them.

"Okay, Daddy," she replied, smiling head-to-toe.

As I snapped that picture, one of those rare moments of fatherhood came into focus, a combination of excitement for her, knowing she was experiencing these smells, sights and sounds for some of the first times, and hope that she would always cherish this as much as I. I was thankful for all that God have given our family. *What a great day.* We loaded up the Mule and headed back down the dike as a flock of woodies got up and flew out, squealing as they cleared the back hedgerow.

"Look, Sarah, at the woodies." I pointed toward the banking birds.

"Can we hunt 'em, Daddy?"

"No, the season's out, Pump Pump."

"Okay, maybe next year."

"Let's go see if Momma has some eggs and bacon ready," I suggested, as we turned through the gate. We rolled back down the farm road straight into the sun, the new morning rays lighting up her soft flushed skin and illuminating her orange toboggan like a beacon. She looked up at me and smiled wide. I wrapped my arm around her and held her tight against my jacket; she cuddled closer. I knew she was growing up and maybe one day wouldn't want to cuddle as close, but that was okay. She would have these memories of the animals, the cold morning air, and her daddy waking her up to go check the traps. And she would soon take her place amongst the photographs in the old store.

My Buddy

Luke's first duck was a drake teal taken in a beaver slough outside of Colerain. He was nine months old, and he brought it straight back, dropped it in my hand, then sat at my feet just like he had done in the backyard. I remember it like it was yesterday, and I don't know who was more proud—me or him.

That was 2001. It had been eight months since I had picked him up after I just happened to read an ad placed in the Raleigh paper. I was smart enough not to take Susan on the first visit to see the litter, but when I took her for the second look, Herb leaned over to me as Susan coddled the yellow puppy, and said, "Ah, I don't know if you know it or not, but you just bought a puppy." He and I have long since become good friends and we still laugh at that remark. But rest assured, the old man knew what he was doing.

After that day, there were so many hunts I can't count them all. They were all good but some of them were just special. There was the time Susan and I took Luke into our impoundment in Maribel. As we packed our gear after the hunt, he kept sprinting back and forth between us and the last cut in the impoundment, each time delivering a teal to our feet and heading back for another. One, two, three, four . . . He kept bringing them one at a time, then returning to the edge of the impoundment for more.

Luke had a terrific nose, and he was tenacious when he smelled a wounded duck. I told Susan they must have been birds she had wounded; she assuredly disagreed. We both laughed and hugged Luke Man. He was as happy as I ever saw him that morning, water splattering all the way from his nose to his tail, as he shook with a wide grin on his face. We loaded up and headed back to Rocky Mount, we in our first year of marriage and he in his warm dog box—relationships sealed.

On the Roanoke in '04, Luke and his momma, Lucy, hunted side by side on a snowy December morning, with a symphony of mallards, widgeon, and teal serenading us all. Amid the falling snow, endless quacking and flapping, and the whooshing of cutting birds, his senses were as full as mine and his golden eyes picked out every flock before I even knew they were there.

Back then, as we got our limit in twenty minutes, he could

jump instantly, effortlessly and repeatedly, from the deer stand perched in the willow. And he could have done it all day.

On another hunt in January of '06, a flock of twelve teal pitched right into our decoys at the mouth of Spencer Bay in Hyde County. After the volley, there were six teal on the water. Before the sixth retrieve, Luke glanced at Herb and me, as if asking doubtfully, "Are you sure there's another one out there pard?" That culled flock of teal is on the wall at the Store now, right near a picture of Sarah hugging the yellow man himself.

• • •

There were two trips to Canada. During one of our first morning hunts, twenty-one mallards folded on the first called shot. At command, Luke barreled into the mayhem of flapping wings, scattering feathers and what must have been duck scent heaven to him. Turning around and around in circles, he momentarily froze. With a confused expression, he looked at me, as if saying, "What the what?" It looked like some type of Lab overload and my laughing echoed over the Saskatchewan plain. He then proceeded to get them all, one at a time.

During those two adventures, he retrieved Canada geese, some almost as big as he, snow geese and, of course, bunches of mallards. He was truly an "international dog." What a spectacle to see hundreds of thousands of birds begin the grand passage up north, a Canadian frost on the peas and an orange sunrise as the backdrop. And topping it off, to have your dog in his prime, nestled close to you, groaning, and whimpering with excitement, as the flocks begin to cup up, searing the air above you. That's a blessing right there.

But Luke was a family dog, too. He was gentle, playful and loving, despite being all business when ducks or doves filled the air. Simply because we answered that ad, Susan, Sarah, and I have met many nice people across eastern North Carolina, and our family has been blessed by many special friendships—all because of one yellow Lab—the only yellow in the litter. He was born the day Susan and I got married and Sarah knew him from birth. As I worked Luke in the back yard during his prime years, Sarah would race him, convinced at three years old that she could beat him to the dummy. He'd give her a head start, but he would always get the dummy. She followed him around the farm from the time she was old enough to walk and would beg him to catch up or demand we slow down as he ran behind our Mule through the farm roads. All the while, she yelled encouragement at the top of her lungs.

When she got older, Sarah would throw the dummy into the water, send him and get somewhat irritated if he tried to bring the dummy to me. Eventually, Luke learned to bring it to her, and he grew to love and probably prefer Sarah's hugs—as well as Susan's babying. If we went to the farm, everybody always wanted to take Luke. He was us.

One of his last great hunts was on Friday afternoon the day before the last day of the 2012–2013 season. It was spitting ice and there was a new rush of ducks in one of our favorite haunts. Luke was the only dog that could go. Herb and I discussed the situation and I thought old yellow boy had one more in him. At 5:00 p.m., we had no ducks. Between 5:00 and 5:20 p.m., we killed our limits. Luke sprang into action and got most of them, repeatedly busting through the ice and cold with me stuffing candy bars into him as fast as I could. After all the ducks were retrieved and gear packed, we began the long wade to the truck. But we didn't have a canoe. Luke had to swim out. We'd done this a hundred times in the past, but that day the cold had taken its toll.

Herb and I took turns carrying Luke out of that frozen swamp; it was a struggle for all three of us. There was no longer the burning desire in Luke's eyes during that journey out of the standing timber—only cold shivering. Packing up the gear and splitting the greenheads, we agreed that was his last day on a hunt like that; the type he lived for. The significance of the moment hit me on the ride home that night. There is unmatched determination in nature: beavers felling trees twice their own diameter and building and re-building dams, salmon somehow finding and heading back up the same streams where they were born after spending years in the ocean, and the very ducks we pursue battling 2,000 miles of winds to arrive at traditional feeding grounds for the winter. But a Lab, especially one past his prime, going into ice to retrieve ducks is as pure as it gets. If you have not seen it, try to do so before you leave this Earth.

Ironically, after spanning North America to retrieve countless species, Luke's last retrieved duck was a coot. Yep, a coot. Sarah begged me to shoot it, as she sat with Luke in a small skiff in the impoundment. I sent old yellow man out of the boat, and he got it, but I knew he was done after that. We shot no more that day. But while picking up decoys, Sarah and I watched squealing woodies and honking geese arrive after shooting hours, silhouetted against a red sunset. A few times, I looked over at my buddy, but there was no excited whimpering nor anticipatory shaking. He observed the birds coming into to roost, landing all around us, but the drive had waned.

I took my time picking up the decoys that evening, watching the woodies and geese glide to stop, listening to the squealing and honking, talking with Sarah and checking on my buddy, hoping to see that old desire in him.

In the fading light, as the January chill took hold, Sarah, Luke, and I slowly made our way down the dike to the Mule. Though he was right there on my left heel like so many times before, a passing had occurred, and I knew it. That was our last hunt with him.

They say a man is lucky to have one good dog. Well, with God's blessing, I've had four. Luke was the third. You would think losing dogs becomes easier after you've been through it a few times. But it's just the opposite. I remember my mother not wanting another bird dog because she didn't want to lose another one. At the vibrant and vigorous age of twenty-four, I didn't understand it. But now I do. We did get another one, after a while.

• • •

Luke is resting now only yards from where Susan and I shot the teal, and where he retrieved the coot for Sarah. Pintails, woodies, teal, and mallards visit him each winter. I know he hears them, smells them, and remembers the good times. And I know he'll always be there, running on the dike.

Rest good, Luke Man. You were a great buddy.

Your buddy,

Bill

October Fields

As you grow older, God has a way of confronting you more and more with your own vulnerability and mortality. In general, you come to realize how fragile life is and how blessed you are to even be here, enjoying family, friends, and the gifts bestowed upon you during your brief time on this earth. Maybe it's just me, but I think you also begin to realize how fortunate we are to live in such a great country, the first country founded by men intent on ensuring that the freedoms they believed were God-given would be preserved. For these beliefs, our Founding Fathers risked everything—families, life, land, fortunes, and liberty. Like all of us, they indeed had flaws as did the fledgling country. Yet, they were shrewd, cunning, determined, and fortuitous—extremely fortuitous.

If you don't think God had a hand in this country's formation, read about the perseverance of George Washington and the Continental Army at Valley Forge in the winter of 1777–1778, and their escape across the East River in the Battle of Long Island. One may say it is just a coincidence and matter of happenstance that the fog rolled into the East River just in time to obscure the fleeing Americans, allowing them to fight another day. Perhaps it can be militarily explained why George Washington, after getting down on his knees and praying for our Army during the bleak days of Valley Forge, gave one of the greatest motivational speeches ever. This speech bolstered their will to hold on until the French pledged to help the young republic in February, thereby setting the stage for the Continental Army to later retake Philadelphia.

But I think fate was involved and I think our leaders believed that theirs was a divine mission. And I believe our leaders were chosen long before the war, tempered by their rearing, their roots, and their experiences. Washington, like many of our best leaders, was a man of the countryside, who stated, "I'd rather be at Mount Vernon with a friend or two about me, than to be attended at the seat of government by the officers of state and the representatives of every power in Europe."

This is one of my favorite quotes from our first president, a reluctant leader thrust into a role for which he genuinely knew he was suited more than any other. Nonetheless, he accepted his fate like one of his mules—stubbornly and ploddingly at first, but with resolute steadfastness once committed. Called by destiny's plan.

I visited Mount Vernon a few years ago with my family. While

Susan and Sarah viewed the garden and gift shops, I slinked off to walk the grounds. I went down the hills to the Potomac River, through the woods, past the mill and beside the corn fields. I wanted to feel the man's presence. As a kindred soul who had also been reared in the country and felt the same pull from a piece of land, I suppose I wanted reassurance from the greatest American that this country would weather its present storms and emerge stronger.

Washington had walked those hills and ravines, peered up into that same tall timber and been nurtured by that soil. I could see why he didn't want to leave this place to fight, sacrificing family, risking his very stake in this new land. It was obvious why he yearned for his maternal farm during the war. I came away that day with a renewed determined outlook, joisted by his inspiring oaks and poplars, and sent forth into my own Valley Forge.

Two years after the Mount Vernon visit, our family traveled to Williamsburg. Not a connoisseur of rides, my only request of Susan and Sarah was that we go to Yorktown. After that, we agreed that Daddy would sit patiently, however long as necessary, as they rode any and all attractions in Bush Gardens or Water Country. *No problem, great deal right there.*

I'd always wanted to visit Yorktown, the site of the decisive battle of the American Revolution. It was where the Americans gained control, and where Cornwallis was finally defeated after marching up through the Carolinas. In recent years, this desire to visit had grown even more.

When we arrived on the grounds and stood beside the

redoubts, I was astounded by how close the battle participants actually engaged each other, only 400 yards across an open field. What it must have been like to see the fire and smoke from the muskets, feel the concussion of the exploding shells, and watch as the British Army withered, its backs against the river; they'd been abandoned by tardy supply ships turned away toward New York by the French, leaving Cornwallis to his own demise. At some point, the Americans must have realized that ultimate victory—defying all odds and contradicting supposedly all-knowing naysayers—was finally theirs.

During those last days in Yorktown's fields and timber, American regulars—who had fought the long years, together with "well-regulated" militia men just off their farms in rural Virginia, and determined to protect their land, alongside our French allies eager to see their visions of a defeated Britain evolve—witnessed the birth of a nation. The militia men had started it all at Lexington and Concord, refusing to allow the British to seize munitions. The regulars then carried us through the darkest and longest days. Now the French, particularly their ships, came to aid the cause—and see it to final victory. We drove around the grounds, stopped at each noted site, listened to the CD purchased at the gift shop, took pictures of the deer, crossed the earthen dam, and visited the Moore House where the terms of surrender were hashed out. We laughed and talked and took it all in as a family. But beneath it all and unnoticed by Susan and Sarah, an immense feeling of respect welled up inside of me. This was the hallowed ground where men's visions of a democratic republic finally became foreseeable reality.

At last, we arrived at the site of the final surrender—Surrender Field, it's aptly called. As I stood there with my family, looking out over the solemn grassy expanse where the British laid down their arms in front of the Americans, I envisioned the troops from both sides gathered in the field to consummate the outcome. The British had just marched all the way from the York River, down a long gravel road surrounded by towering oaks and maples on either side; reverent botanical witnesses playing host to one of the great historic performances. The Americans had lined each side of the road, forming a gauntlet only feet from the men they had just bombed, charged and tried to eviscerate. Now, a sense of civility once again prevailed. Yet, it must have been such an emotional moment for our soldiers. The greatest army in the world was marching by them, faces forward—not wanting to look the Americans in the eye. The once-confident British were now properly and obligatorily poised to surrender to the allied forces of France's established army, the American Continental Army, and to the ever-ready militia men from the local area. I could almost hear the clanging of swords and the marched rustle of polished leather boots on the gravel, and the subtle orders being given by stoic commanders.

What a scene it must have been: the brilliant blue coats of the Americans and the French, the stark garnet-red dress of the British, the walnut and blued metal muskets laid back over weary but excited shoulders, the cannons in perfect line, the drums beating a slow rhythmic decisive beat, the subdued contriteness of the British, the hidden but chesty exuberance of the Americans, the pride of the French, the eventual slap of hands against locks, stocks and barrels as they were laid down . . . and enveloping it all, the lingering aroma of spent gunpowder among mid-October's yellowing leaves. I could feel the excitement our troops must have felt, for they knew they were soon to embark on an experiment in freedom—victorious after all those years. What these trees and this land must have witnessed! It was an honor to stand there with my wife and daughter. I gave silent but resolute thanks, as I looked up into the oaks and over the field.

I do believe this determination and perseverance is still here in this land today. You do not see it much because for some unknown reason, many would rather watch celebrities exhibit their dysfunctional lives or play video games. I suppose those activities turn the almighty dollar more than ensuring we know our history. But there are certain people in this land who understand the importance of what has been sacrificed, both at Yorktown and in other battles on this soil and overseas. These ordinary, sincere, genuine people like you can preserve for our children the country fought for and won by those men at Yorktown. It would be easy to look at all the negatives facing this country now and give up. Likewise, it would have been easy for the troops at Valley Forge facing freezing cold with no food and no shoes to give up in December 1777. But they did not, and because of that, there was Yorktown. There is another Yorktown out there in our country's future. I may not be here to see it; I may only see this continued Valley Forge, or perhaps a Battle of Long Island or maybe a Saratoga or Kings Mountain. But there is a Yorktown. If you do not believe it, go walk around the redoubts of that battlefield or through the ravines of Mount Vernon, or go stand in line and look again at the Declaration of Independence and recommit yourself. It's up to us to find it. Eight years after that battle on the York River in Virginia, we were given the freedoms to do so by the Constitution.

As our family drove away from Yorktown that day, Sarah asked, "Daddy, how did they all know the battle was going to take place in Yorktown?"

What a question, I thought, soaking in one of those special moments of fatherhood, knowing it would be shadowed soon by swooping rides, loop-de-loops and water blasters. Wanting to take advantage of such an opportunity, I paused. "Well, Sarah, they didn't really know it, it's just where everyone ended up and converged in a moment of time. In this case, a very historic moment in time determined mostly by geography." I went on to explain some other important points, as I saw them. *Maybe some of them hit home?*

None of us really knows where the next Yorktown will be, but when it happens, we need to understand that it is indeed happening and relish the destiny. It is our obligation to those who stood victorious on that gravel road in 1781. I leave you with another of my favorite quotes from Washington: "There is a Destiny which has the control of our actions, not to be resisted by the strongest efforts of Human Nature." It was said by him in 1758, eighteen years before the Declaration of Independence was signed.

Signs

Before the days of radar apps, hour-by-hour delineations of expected barometric changes, satellite channels and podcasts staffed with frothing hyperbolic pronouncers of the obvious describing the possibility of a one-inch snowstorm in International Falls, Minnesota, like it was the 1980 Olympic hockey victory, we relied mostly on the local "weatherman" to tell us what was coming. He was done in five minutes, and he didn't spend ten minutes telling us what he was going to tell us five minutes later. His delivery was professional, but he usually wasn't all that accurate in terms of when, how much, and where the snow would fall.

In 1973, we had a snowstorm that stayed on the ground a week and they didn't call off school any of those days until 7:00 a.m. each morning, presumably because they were unsure what the overnight temperatures had been and how the roads had faired. Back in the day, it seemed the old timers I grew up around were just as accurate as the three guys on the local TV stations, if not more so.

In the winter of '69, Granddaddy shuffled into the Store one morning and proclaimed, "Feels like snow out there."

"It sure does, Mr. Clyde," Mom replied.

I excitedly sprang up from my regular Saturday morning position behind the counter. Back in those days, before I started carrying a shotgun or fishing at the river on my own, I relied more on the AccuMom forecast than the TV men. "Is it going to snow today Mom?" I blurted.

"I believe so, Billy. The weatherman in Greenville says there's a good chance."

l checked the cardboard Daisy box on the shelf behind the cash register, a source of increased cash flow from the local boy population during the winter. It was full of the slim ten-cent BB packages, so I obligingly grabbed a few and stuffed them into my jacket pocket. "I'm going to the house to get my boots and go BB gun hunting!" I hollered to Mom, as I ran out the front door of the store.

As predicted by Granddaddy, the first flakes started later that morning. A potato, corn, and bean farmer, Granddaddy knew well the signs of weather. His livelihood had relied on them for sixty years by that time. I don't profess to be as accurate as Granddaddy, or even Mom, but I too can usually smell the snow in the air; I know I feel it in my bones more these days. To those of us who have relished the outdoors in these parts, that heavy biting cold combined with a northwest wind and a low gray sky that signals a pending snow event is something we know well. Maybe it's not as well-timed nor well-documented, and maybe it's not as good a predicter as a Jim Cantore visit to the area, but we trust our gut. These shifts are definite signs—solid, dependable, and true—backed by substantial gray hairs on our heads that many winters ago were once brown bangs trapped under our red wool caps.

Back in '69, when AccuMom said it was going to snow, a nine-year-old boy didn't need an illustration of the low front turning north up the coast with a northwest wind coming in behind it. It was a sure bet that soon at my grandmamma's house, the chickadees would be scrambling, the cardinals would be fluffing their vivid red against the inundated white pine branches and, although I didn't know it at the time, maybe the cedar waxwings would be down.

That first winter of my BB-gun hunting days, the cedar waxwings mysteriously just appeared one morning. The hunting exploits of most of us boys in the community had only consisted of a few months, and none of us had ever seen the brown-feathered, cardinal-shaped birds with the light green patches under their throats. But for two weeks, we were infatuated, watching them twirl and bob upside down, while trying to pluck blue berries from the local bushes that went by some name that I never could remember. We just called them bushes, and Mom said she thought the birds got drunk on those blueberries. I'm not so sure she wasn't correct. Whatever the issue, they'd turn upside down and swarm all over the large shrubs, pushing each other aside, fluttering to another limb, then realigning with a new group. I never saw anything else like it again until I hunted early mallards in Saskatchewan and saw one tornado after another swoop down to feed on the peas.

The waxwings were an amazing sight for a boy who was just becoming accustomed to the thrills of hunting wild creatures. From then on, when winter approached, I looked for the first signs of the tweeting flocks of birds flying between the gum trees and the shrubs. But for some reason, the hordes of cedar waxwings never came back. They'd show up in small flocks, maybe ten or twelve here and there, but not in the flocks of fifty that had swarmed down and voraciously consumed all the berries. I've only seen that one time in my life and that was when I was nine years old.

I still look up in the air when I hear that unique tweeting the cedar waxwing emits and, to me, it's a sign that winter has arrived. Actually, nature usually gives us ample notice of upcoming events, if we pay attention. The first blows of September are a sign that mullets will soon school up in the local rivers. When the flocks of white swans cry overhead, making their mid-morning journey from the Sound to the wheat fields, we all know that winter is settling. Bushytails get a push to start planning their annual frantic burying when the clusters of white oak acorns fill the treetops.

Of course, there are also signs and clues that subtly try to tantalize us with captive secrets. Why do the ducks show up in the same spot year after year, after flying thousands of miles? Biologists have studied this for years and there are all kinds of explanations, including the postulate that little bits of magnetite in their brain help guide them. Or perhaps they orient themselves to the Big Dipper or align their path to some other stars in the clear winter sky? Personally, I probably buy the magnetite theory more than any others, but I can tell you that once they find a food source, the word gets out. I'm not sure there's a duck language that offers the conjugation of any particular verb; however, I can tell you that they do have their own exclamations and the excited word spreads fast among them when there's smartweed, wild aquatic rice, or flooded corn on the menu. There are other indications all around us that are perhaps even more perplexing. While in college, I spent a summer hacking through the Carolina bays in southeastern North Carolina. Our job, funded via a grant through the university, was to hike into to the center of these bays and take samples of the peat that had accumulated under the thick vegetation. There was an energy crisis affecting the country and we were charged with documenting any minable peat deposits. If you don't know, Carolina bays are shallow elliptical depressions in the coastal plains of North Carolina, Georgia, South Carolina, and other states. Their axes are elongated northwest to southeast. How they were formed is still a mystery.

In those days, many believed meteorites had something to do with it while recent theories of origin include the effects of prevailing winds on sand dunes during ice ages. But if you look at them in aerial photos, they do have the distinct impression of being formed by a splattering meteorite. Regardless, their formation is still a mystery. I'm not sure their origin will ever be fully explained. Sometimes, nature holds onto her secrets just so we can realize that we may not be as smart as we think we are. Why does that salmon return to its birth stream after several years in the ocean? How does that baby murre gather up the courage to hurl itself off a northern sea cliff hundreds of feet high where it was hatched and raised, and then bravely spread its wings on a perilous glide to the ocean? We may never know the answers. I think God designed it that way. These are just a very few of the mysteries in this world that we cannot fully comprehend. There are many more, and though I am forever intrigued by those riddles, many hints that there may be more to this existence than we might expect are not simply relegated to animal behaviors. If we pay close attention, these signs are shown to us; fleeting yes, but definitely present—rare clues that there's more around us than we know. There are some things that are simply undeniable, that cannot be legitimately or logically reasoned by some algorithm or experiment. No matter how much one may desire to intellectually hypothesize a particular scenario or rationalize that there's no proof that a higher authority or divine power is active in our daily lives, it sometimes becomes extremely difficult to deny that we humans simply do not have all the answers.

...

During my late thirties and early forties, I regularly duck hunted in a beaver slough in Bertie County, North Carolina. The property was owned by a friend and one-time customer of mine, whom I'd met when I was in the banking business. One day after a business discussion, he'd invited me to hunt anytime in this slough that was situated behind his chicken houses at the confluence of two creeks. He'd hunted it hard in the '70s with one of his buddies, but it hadn't been hunted at all in twenty years. Seeing the potential for a virgin duck haven, I promptly took him up on his offer. Standing in that flooded mecca among the willows and oaks, I learned how to work circling mallards, shot my first banded greenhead, and saw everything from teal to gadwall to widgeon suck into decoys. When the wind was out of the north and the snow moved the birds off the Chowan, it was a great place to be.

Although subsequent moves with my career took me to various towns in eastern North Carolina, I continued to hunt that pond.

One January morning, I decided to get up and drive an hour and a half from where I was living to see if I could coerce some greenies once again. An extremely hard wind from the northwest had brought much rain and as I arrived in the early morning darkness at the edge of the woods that kept the pond hidden, I quickly noticed several trees had blown down during the storm.

Starting down the narrow path to the beaver pond, I immediately had to start dodging rearranged branches and broken limbs. As I was prone to do back then, I was rushing and stupidly forgot to zip up my backpack. About a third of the way to the slough, a huge poplar had blown down across the path. Thick briars and reeds covered the areas to either side, so the only solution was to get down on my hands and knees and crawl under the tree. Frustrated with the delay, I hastily discarded my decoy sack and threw it under the tree but kept my pack on my back. I scampered through the small opening relatively easily but, as I came out the other side, I heard unsettling rattles clanging down my back. All my gear hit the ground in a concerted splash, thump, and crash. In the periphery of my headlamp, I could see knives, flashlights, snacks, calls, and other essentials scattering into the weeds around me. "Dern it!" I shouted. *Now I'm late, all my gear is on the ground and who knows what other obstacles await me on this path!*

I quickly scoured the ground, scooping up all the dumped items I could see. I threw them in the pack and zipped up the pockets. Of course, I wasn't too happy about the incident and murmured some choice words while I was doing it. Hoisting all my gear on my back, I scooted off again down the path—now at double-time.

Reaching the pond at first light, I immediately splashed into the middle, put a hook on a tree, slung my pack onto it, hung the Remington on the hook and commenced to throwing out the decoys. Two hours passed and a couple of woodies got fooled. Other than that, it was slow. I decided that I'd eat a snack and wait another thirty minutes before leaving. After all, there was plenty of work waiting for me back at the office.

As any duck hunter knows, if you want ducks to appear, just start making plans to go potty, start eating, or just don't look in the air. Accordingly, I kept an eye turned up, as I reached to get my pack down. As I grasped the pack, it predictably slipped through my hands and quickly ended up completely upside down in the water. Only then did I realize that in my haste, I hadn't zipped up the middle compartment! You guessed it, all the pack's contents cascaded right out of the pack and straight into the pond.

Lickity-split, done, dropped, wet. The dumped gear most certainly included my knife, flashlight, snacks and the most important thing—my father's watch! Back then, I habitually wore my father's watch, even when I hunted. Daddy's watch was a thin, vintage 1940s Hamilton wind-up gold watch that my mother gave to me when I graduated from college. She'd kept if for me without my knowledge. I promptly took it to a jeweler in New Bern, who fixed the broken springs, put a shiny gold band on it and polished it to its original brilliance. I wore the watch with much pride, and it was the focus of many inquiries from friends and acquaintances.

When I was young, it was an adornment that aided my welcoming into the world of adulthood and into the professional world of business. I wore it not only at the office and during social interactions, but also while hunting. It meant a lot to me. My dad was an avid hunter—mostly quail—and it was another connection to him. I knew it wasn't wise to wear it in such risky environments as beaver ponds, but rather than leave it in the truck, I chose to store it in the pack so I could check the time. This was before reliable "smart" cell phones, so I didn't have a phone with me. I had one back in my truck, but I didn't have a cell phone that I carried around with me. As the bag spilled all its contents into the pond, I was horrified that my watch was now buried in the mucky bottom. I accepted that it would probably never work again, but I did want to find it. For twenty minutes, I searched and flailed around the mucky bottom, hoping I would be lucky enough to find the watch. Finally—dejected and ashamed—I decided to pack up all my gear and head out. By this time, the sun had risen enough that it was gradually winning over what had been a dreary morning, announcing its arrival with streaming intermittent spears of light cutting through the woods and showering the slough. The morning was rapidly warming. I gathered up my decoys, zipped up the top of the pack good this time, threw the gun over my shoulder, grabbed my walking stick, and headed out.

Stepping out on the bank of the beaver pond, I hesitated and retraced everything. *You know, just maybe the watch fell out of the pack on the way in that morning. It had been dark, and yes, I'd been in a hurry. There was a possibility, albeit a very small possibility, that the watch had fallen out of the pack onto the path.* It was a stretch, but I clung to it. Not very practiced in prayer at the time, I took a sincere moment—right there on the edge of the pond—and asked that my idiocy be forgiven and that the watch somehow be there in the woods. It was an emotional moment. I felt terrible that I'd been so careless as to drop into a beaver pond the gift my mother had given me, that indeed my dad had left me, and that they'd both entrusted to me. I was not sixteen anymore. I was forty years old, and I thought I was smarter than that. *Nope.* I began my guilt-ridden trudge out. Each side of the path was scanned and re-scanned as the truck got closer and closer. I wasn't expecting to find the watch, but I kept hoping and continuing to pray that somehow it had slipped out of the pack—all the while knowing that the best chance I'd have to find it would be near where I'd crawled under the poplar.

The sun continued its climb; its rays of light shone through the tops of the trees onto the path, dimpling the forest with brief little spectacles, like lightning bugs dancing on a July evening. The thrushes began to skirt from bush to bush and the squirrels were starting to shower me from above, as they catapulted from tree to tree on the way to their stored food locations—each species signaling the formal end of the storm in its own way. I kept a silent prayer wedged somewhere between the supposed intellectual part of my brain and the more mystic folds that clung to the last threads of idealistic dogma. Desperation battled logic and logic fought my last wishful remnants of hope. *Bill, how could you be so stupid. Idiot! Please God . . . let me find that watch. Let me find that watch.* But I secretly knew the chances of it being there were miniscule. It was a shameful combination of jumbled self-criticizing and sporadic utterances shrouded in a very slight glimmer of feigned optimism, mixed with heartfelt prayer. As I rounded the corner in the trail and spotted the blow-down up ahead at approximately forty yards, my eyes were re-directed toward the right side of the path. Just on my side of the blowdown, something was reflecting the intruding rays. My first thought was that an old can or a piece of farm machinery that I'd never noticed had suddenly been found by the emerging sun that was reclaiming its day. The morning was growing clearer by the minute and the sun had just then found its precise angle to reflect directly off whatever the object was. It seemed odd to me that at this exact moment I approached, the sun was shining it brightest. Whatever was on the ground was reflecting stronger and stronger. This was no normal reflection. It was a brilliant, sparkling announcement, demanding to be noticed—a vivid pronounced presence in an otherwise uniform forest. Peering closer among the dapples of light, I became transfixed on the illuminated object. *Certainly, that could not be my watch? There's no way that is my watch, shining that brightly, begging to be noticed. That just couldn't happen!*

But the other side of my brain frantically grasped at the possibility that the object might be my watch. *Could it be? But what are the chances that I fell down, the watch fell out, it landed at that exact place so that the sun was now reflecting off it just as I returned at the precise right moment for all this to happen?*

Educated in science at a major university, the logical part of my brain began to perform its skeptic duties on what was left of my child-like beliefs. *No way, that's not your watch, you idiot! You've simply screwed up, bud. You've dumped your father's watch in the pond . . . lost it. It's that simple. You've learned a hard lesson . . . at forty.*

But the idealistic boyish Bill still held out for a miracle; the same Bill that unlike the rest of the family, had stayed in the den one February day in 1974 to witness the final seconds of the A.C.C. game of week. I was rewarded then by seeing the Heels come from eight points down with seventeen seconds left to beat the Blue Devils. So, I still had a chance. Maybe I could sink a forty-footer like Sweet D? Forty yards turned into twenty yards. I remained glued to that reflection, zeroing in on it like a heron on a minnow. Either the sun was not moving, or the reflection was that strong, but that brilliant light did not change. The exact angle remained and the object, whatever it was, continued to project its presence right at me. I'm no fan of physics. I disliked the subject in school and I'm sure that somebody versed in the laws of prism refraction could tell me why that reflection stayed bright, as I walked right up to it. But it was a curiosity then and still is today. As I got to ten yards, I realized the object was golden in color. *That's what the watch would look like!* I eased ahead even more; the ten yards turned to seven yards. "It couldn't be the watch. It has to be some kind of gold-colored piece of metal that's been misplaced in these woods," I openly muttered to myself, hoping the squirrels wouldn't hear my mumbling and agree. "That cannot be my father's watch!"

I eased up, seeing the side of a band. "No!" I disbelieved, edging closer. "Is that glass on top? Could that be the crystal? No, it can't be!" I stood at three yards . . . and froze. There it was—the gold Hamilton was laying perfectly in a weed patch, with the crystal exposed toward the sun. It was as if somebody had gently placed it there, facing my direction. There was no way I could miss it. I stood there motionless among the pines, the Remington slung over my shoulder, decoys covering the shivers traveling down my back. I stared at the watch, its precious metal shining up at me. Slowly, I raised my head toward the canopy with a thankful acknowledgment. The sun had been pushing its way through a single small hole between the maples and pines, a minute opening that within the next five minutes would be past its point of relevance.

Transfixed, I followed the tiny ray of sunlight from the canopy down to the watch. The small dapple was only covering a two-square-foot piece of ground, and my watch was signaling its presence right in the middle of it—shining its message just to me. I threw off my decoys, took off my wet pack, and dropped to a knee. Still in disbelief, I picked up the watch and held it. It was ticking its precise antique rhythm, like I was sitting at my desk with it wrapped snugly on my wrist. Thankfully, I gazed up to the canopy again, gathering in the moment. I couldn't believe that I'd found it, that a tree had blocked the path for the first time ever that day, causing me to climb under it. And because I'd climbed under that tree for the first time ever going to that beaver pond, the mistake I'd made by leaving my pack unzipped enabled me to spill the contents onto the path. What had irritated me as I'd scrambled under the poplar at 5:00 a.m. that morning now made me voluminously happy. It struck me with total awe what had just happened.

On the way back to the truck, I'd arrived there at the precise time that the sun had found my watch. From forty yards away, I'd been drawn to it; the sign was obvious, like a beacon from a castaway on a deserted island. I stayed there on my knees for several minutes. I can't explain all the feelings I had, but I can tell you that there was a reaffirmation in me that there's more to life than what we understand. Yeah, yeah, I know. I had the same thoughts then. *It's just a coincidence, Bill. Yep. The fact that you crawled under this tree for the first time and spilled your watch out onto that path preventing it from later falling into beaver pond, and the fact that you happened to walk out at the exact time that the canopy happened to be open to the perfectly correct angle of sunlight, and that the only ray of light in that area had struck your watch at the specific right time when you returned—it was all just a coincidence.* That was the B.S. degree in me, trying to sliver its way back into the twenty-one-year-old total devotee of Darwin that it once knew. But it wasn't successful.

I stayed there on my knee, fastening the watch back on my left wrist where it belonged and had been destined to be since 1962. You can say that emotions won out over logic that day. You can even say I was downright illogical for thinking my thoughts that day. You can say that it's simply a matter of the psychological aspects of one's emotions taking over the normal logical thought processes because of one's prior disposition to believe such an event is possible. I'm sure there are all kinds of arguments one can make that would counter what I felt that day. I understand that. That's fine if some people want to make those arguments. I'm okay with all that. So be it. But I was there. In my mind, there's no other explanation for all these coincidences surrounding something as important as that watch, and I can tell you that on my knee in that pine woods that day, I had a connection with my father that I will never be able to explain. It was a sign.

Such an example has happened to me one other time. I'm fully aware of all the arguments that a psychiatrist or skeptic would make against my interpretation of the first instance and of the one I'm about to share. But the study of the brain and human emotions is really in its infancy. Do we truly understand the more complex functions of the brain? I don't mean the electrical impulses and neuro this or cerebral that. I mean, the intricate emotional workings.

In my younger days, I might have made the same argument

that many would make against my feelings surrounding these happenings. Who knows, maybe the skeptics are right? I'm sure there's a way to argue their point just to win the debate. But it won't be won with me. I lived them. My mother passed away in 1999. The first week after her death, I stayed with my stepfather going through items at the house, getting accounts straight and settling the estate the best we could those first few days.

The following week, I went back to work and tried to catch up with customers and take care of my regular duties, but I was not totally into it. As a matter of fact, a good friend of mine called me that week and told me that after he had lost his mother, he really didn't feel like he was productive until six months had passed. Ironically, it would be six months to the day before I felt that way. But in that second week, I was trying my best to get it done. I was single at the time, living alone, and kept everything at my home in neat order as I thought it should be. Of course, those were the days before I was married and had a child, so I had my own idea of order that I always thought was correct. This, I learned later— after marital education and the Manchurian realignment of my pre-wedding beliefs—wasn't even close to reality. One day during that week, I came home for lunch to relax and take a few minutes to forget about lending money and production goals, and step back from the grueling task of handling my mother's affairs. I'd planned to relax in my chair, eat a sandwich and get my mess right. As I walked through the living room on the way to the bedroom—like I'd done hundreds of times before—I glanced over to the bookcase at the edge of the fireplace, and abruptly stopped.

This bookcase rose several feet up toward the apex of a vaulted ceiling. On its shelves, I kept many of my favorite books and, on the lowest shelf and upon two unsteady stands, I'd placed two pictures. One was a picture of my father, holding a quail with a pointer reaching for it, its front paws hugging my father's chest. It was out of a newspaper where my uncle had worked in the 1950s. Daddy had his Winchester double barrel slung over his shoulder. The caption read, *Carroll Fentress with his fine young retriever.* On the other stand was a picture of my mother. My eyes were riveted to the picture of my father, except I couldn't see him. I could only see the frame and the paper backing of the picture. The wire that had been installed by the framer so it could be hung from a wall was clearly visible, as the picture sat in the stand—backwards. I just stared at it. A tingle raced down my back and the hair on my neck started to rise. I certainly hadn't left the picture like that. *Did I turn the picture around when I'd dusted two weeks ago? No, I didn't turn that picture around backwards! I would never do that, while dusting a million times. Somebody must have broken in!* I surmised. Quickly, my eyes glanced around the room. *TV there. Stereo there. Nothing disturbed on the bookcase . . . nothing disturbed around the room.*

  I rushed into the bedroom and searched the closet; all my firearms were where I'd left them. I ran upstairs and looked in the second bedroom closet; all firearms were there, also. Nothing had been altered. I quickly ran back down the stairs and zoomed in on the picture across the room once again; it was still turned around in the stand. *Nothing in the living room, nothing in the dining room, nothing in the kitchen . . . nothing disturbed.* The living room was quiet as I stood there, eliminating possibilities.

Again, I rushed into my bedroom. The .357 I always kept in the nightstand drawer was right where I'd left it that morning. I checked the back door. *Locked.* I checked the side door. *Locked.* I checked the front door. *Locked.* All windows were locked. I circled back to the living room and stood there, glaring at the picture. My mind raced, searching for an explanation. *Maybe my girlfriend at the time had come over to clean up as a favor to me? That's it.* I called her. "Hey sweetie, have you been in my house?" I asked. She had a key, and it would have been fine.

"No, Bill, I haven't been over there since before your mom passed away." I could feel the shiver creeping up my back again. "Why are you asking?"

"I don't really know how to say this but the picture of my father in the stand behind my chair is turned around, so that the back of it faces out into the living room? That stand is so precarious, you know?"

"Yes, definitely, but nobody's broken in the house, right?"

"I don't think so, but I am confused," I stated. Saying goodbye, I hung up the phone, walked over to the bookcase and examined the picture like an enigmatic mystery box. I turned it around in my hands, and there it was—the picture of my father holding the quail, just like it had always been.

After repositioning it with the picture facing outward, I walked over to the middle of the living room and slowly turned back around. For some reason, I fully expected to see it facing backwards in the stand again. I can't explain why, but there was such of an eerie feeling in that room that I didn't know what was possible or impossible. It was just as I had placed it. I couldn't reason, interpolate or titrate how this had occurred, but I came to the temporary conclusion that there was no explanation.

As I prepared my salad, I continually glanced at the bookcase. Then I took a seat in my chair right in front of the picture. Although the news was blaring, I wasn't watching it. Instead, I thought about what had transpired over the last week, and what was remaining to be done with the lawyers, the accounts and the banks; how my sister and I would now have to help manage what would probably become loneliness for my stepfather. All this was weighing on me heavily. I turned around. The picture was still there, facing in the right direction. I went back to work, talked to customers, worked out some loan deals, and plodded through the afternoon while my mind drifted to my mother and stepfather and the past week. I continually wondered about the picture on the bookcase.

In a hurry to get home, I bolted from work at 5:00 p.m. sharp, which was unusual for me. I quickly unlocked the side door, walked in, and immediately honed my stare toward the picture. It was there alright, facing toward me, just as it should have been. I threw the keys on the table, walked over, and glared down at it, wondering how in the world that picture had been turned around. I couldn't understand. There was no reason it should have been in that position. *Nobody had been in the house. I hadn't disturbed it. No alarm had gone off. Nobody had broken in and all the keys were in the right places. Nothing was stolen. Nobody would come in and just turn a picture around, right? Bill don't let your emotions get away with you, bud. There's a logical reason for all this. Somebody broke into the house, evaded the alarm and left. It didn't work. You'd turned the picture around when you dusted and didn't notice it for two weeks.* That made no sense at all. Dumbfounded, I stood there in my suit. *Was this some sort of sign I didn't understand? No Bill, you're scientifically educated. You've made a career out of analyzing loans, cash flows, EBITDA, and inventory turns, and closing those loans if the concrete numbers worked. If they don't fit the parameters, you don't book the business. Black and white, simple . . . purely logical work dictated by policies, regimens, and experiences.* There had to be a reasonable explanation for the picture being turned around.

But as much as I tried, standing there in my living room, and just like in the woods on my knees, I had no logical explanation for the turned around picture . . . or for the gold watch appearing on the path. Don't get me wrong, I believe there are explanations. I just wouldn't call them logical.

All around us there are signs of many things. That big old buck will leave a track if you know where to look, and if you know how to determine how fresh it is, you may want to put that stand up and catch him walking to his scrape. That playful otter will leave telltale sign on the bank where he's crossed, complete with crayfish scales. Turkeys will leave a track and, if you look close enough, you'll see where the long middle prong signals it is an old longbeard and not a hen. Likewise, his wing scrapes on a dirt road will let the sharp hunter know where he's strutting. If you wade and carefully scout a beaver pond, sometimes you can see feathers; and if you look close enough, you can determine if they're wood ducks using in there, or the greenheads that you really want to see. These are all valid proven signs that you can hold in your hand and verify with your mind.

They are concrete and repetitive indications of things that excite us. But I've come to believe there are other signs that are out there too—signs akin to the ducks being able to navigate in the dark and showing up every year at the same place, akin to swans coming to the same fields year after year from thousands of miles away. Is it just a coincidence that the arrangement of our solar system resembles the makeup of an atom? Yes, there are signs that there's a higher power out there. Oh, I'm sure some people don't believe in God and that's fine. It's their choice. But how one can pay attention and study some of the real mysteries in this world, and still not believe there's a higher power, is beyond me. I know I certainly do.

I'm stubborn and it's had to be proven to me over many years. But just as I paid attention to those splayed tracks with accompanying dew claw marks in the damp farm fields and downy feathers floating on beaver ponds in my younger days, I realize now that there may also be signs that some things in this world perhaps are not explainable by the mere ignorant beings we exhibit to be. These days, I'm more acutely aware of the real science all around us that may not be easily illustrated with a theorem or equation, but nonetheless breaks through the walls of human narcissism and perceived correctness to tweak us in the direction of a truer meaning. Maybe it took a ray of sunlight blasting down through a canopy and perhaps a turned-around picture a week after my mom's death, but I got the message. I saw the signs.

ACKNOWLEDGMENTS

I want to thank my editor, Steven Manchester for his guidance, expertise, and inspiration. Steve, not only did you offer your time and suggestions in the editing process, but most importantly, you were encouraging from the first time we talked. For that, I owe you much. Thank you, sir.

Thank you Barbara Aronica-Buck and Jeremy Townsend for your help respectively in designing and copyediting. It was a pleasure working with you both.

I also want to thank Candy Sutton for her sketches contained in this book. Candy, in your art, you brought to life my memories. The River Road, especially, is how I remember it. Thank you for your help, hard work and support.

Thank you Will Primos for your Foreword, and for your feedback and support. You are truly a credit to our traditions and heritage, and it has been a pleasure working with you and getting to know you, sir.

Finally, I want to thank Mrs. Belle Taylor, my high school English teacher, who first encouraged me in my writing, and who gave me the confidence to write with my heart at Carolina, and beyond.

Thank you for purchasing and reading *The Yellow Honeysuckle is the Sweetest*. I hope you enjoyed it, as that is my barometer of true success. If you are willing, I would very much appreciate your sharing it with friends and family, and leaving an online review on Amazon. My plan is to write more, and reviews posted online will help ensure that is possible. Other updates are available at billfentress.com.

Thank you again for your willingness to be part of my journey.

Bill Fentress

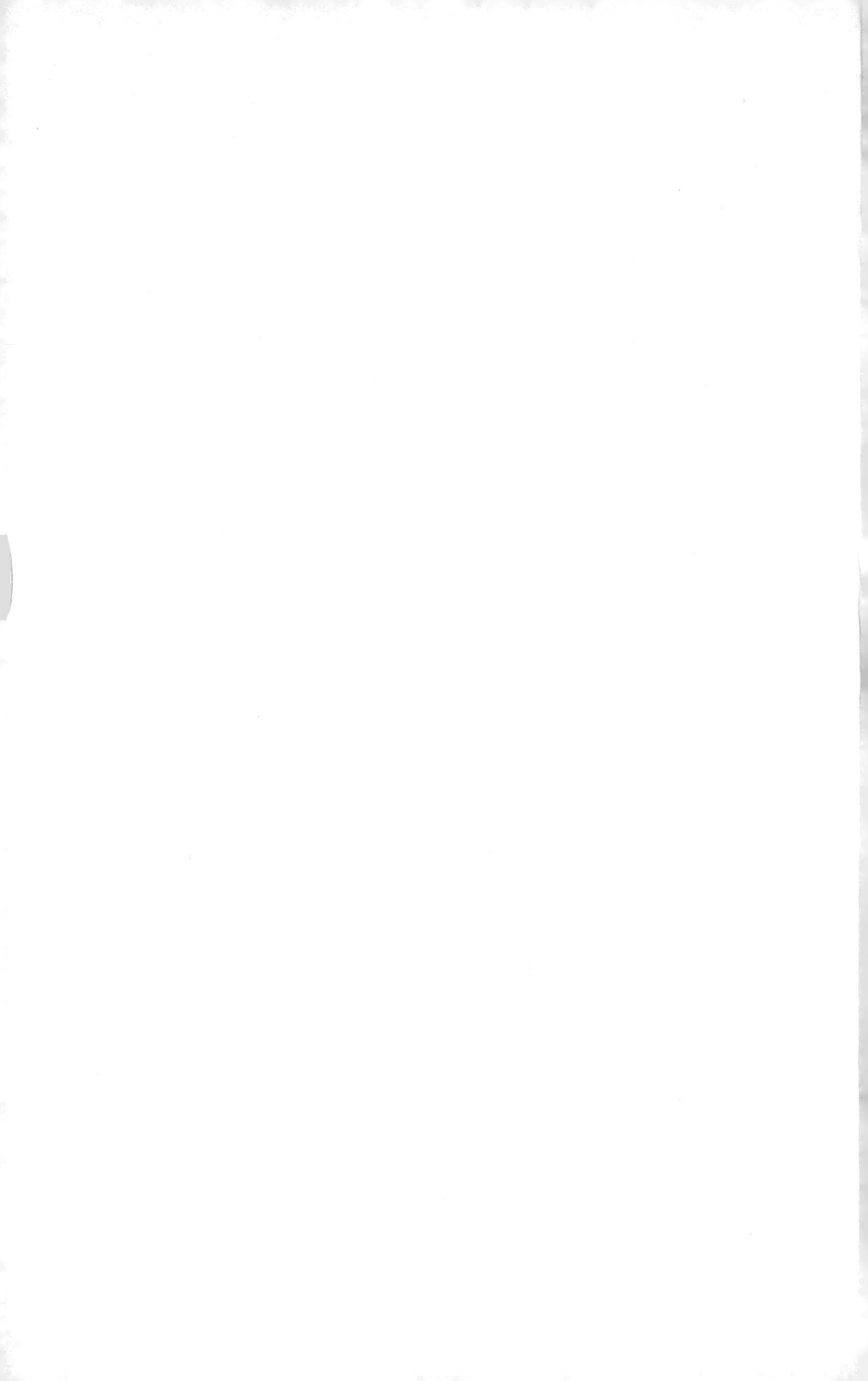